365

BE RTIME STORIES

Dennis McCloskey

Published by

 GENERAL STORE
PUBLISHING HOUSE

1 Main Street, Burnstown, Ontario, Canada K0J 1G0
1-800-465-6072 or Fax: (613) 432-7184

ISBN 0-919431-21-6
Printed and bound in USA.

Cover design and illustrations by Bill Slavin
Production and assembly by Hugh Malcolm

Copyright © 1989
The General Store Publishing House
Burnstown, Ontario, Canada

Canadian Cataloguing in Publication Data

McCloskey, Dennis, 1948-
    365 beertime stories
ISBN 0-919431-21-6

    1. Beer–Anecdotes. 2. Beer–Humor I. Title.
PN6268.B4M33 1989   641.2'3'0207   C89-090207-0

First Printing October 1989

Second Printing April 1990

Third Printing May 1995

"Did you ever taste beer?"
"I had a sip of it once," said the small servant.
"Here's a state of things!" cried Mr. Swiveller.
"She NEVER tasted it — it can't be tasted in a sip!"

— *Charles Dickens,*
  The Old Curiosity Shop (1841)

For Kris,
who has sipped
—but never tasted—
beer.

FROM THE AUTHOR

"I put things down on sheets of paper and stuff them in my pockets, when I have enough, I have a book."

— *John Lennon*

For years, I have been collecting stories, jokes, poems, anecdotes, tall tales and facts pertaining to one of the world's oldest and best-loved beverages.

I now have enough for a book.

It was published for beer drinkers who enjoy this golden, frothy, thirst-quenching beverage the only way it should be consumed — in moderation.

Connoisseurs of beer never guzzle. They savour the flavour. So, drink responsibly and gently. And when you drive, have none for the road!

Dennis McCloskey
1989

1 New York Giants Manager John J. McGraw guided his baseball team to two consecutive World Series victories over the Yankees in 1921 and 1922. At one point, McGraw told his ballplayers that it was a sign of good luck if they could spot a beer wagon before going to the game. McGraw then hired a driver to haul a wagon outside the ballpark when he knew his players would be arriving for an important game in the World Series. His team won. McGraw then hired the driver for the rest of the series and the Giants won every game. Known as "Little Napoleon", McGraw managed the Giants to ten major league pennant victories from 1904-1924.

2 The greatest collection of different British beer labels is 27,845. Keith Osborne is the proud collector and his oldest label is from D.B. Walker & Co., Warrington. The beer label was printed around 1846.

3 In her former role as wife of Canada's ambassador to the U.S., Sondra Gotlieb often related tales of woe about being a Canadian in Washington. She said Americans know Canada for its three M's — Mounties, mountains and Molson's.

4 You can always tell drinkers of imported beer. But you can't tell them much.

5 The Norwegian captain of a Dutch whaler that capsized as it was trying to pull aboard a giant whale went down with his ship while holding a beer in his hands, survivors reported. The 42-member crew of the 543-ton factory ship Tonna, landed at Funchal, Madeira, after being picked up by a Greek freighter when the whaler floundered about 220 miles off the Portuguese coast. The crew said the last thing they saw before the ship went down was Captain Vesprhein, 52, clinging to his bridge with a beer to his lips. They implored him to abandon ship but he refused.

6 Pat Murphy worked at the local brewery. One day while stirring a vat of beer he lost his balance and fell in. Pat's wife was called to the brewery and given the awful news of his drowning. After regaining her composure, she commented that his death was probably merciful and quick. The foreman shook his head, saying: "I don't know about that Mrs. Murphy. He got out twice to go to the bathroom."

7 When several vats in a London, England brewery were struck by lightning, not only were the containers undamaged, but the beer in them was found to have improved considerably in quality. This is believed to be the first recorded case of a storm actually brewing.

8 Little Simon Barwell, of Carlton, England, planted a sunflower but it just wouldn't grow no matter how much he watered it. The youngster then poured some of his father's home-brewed beer on the plant out of sheer desperation. The plant grew to a height of more than 12 feet.

9 Paul Galegos, of Idaho, found out the hard way that you can lead a snake to beer but you can't make it drink. Paul tapped his friend's pet rattlesnake on the head in an attempt to pour beer through the snake's mouth, but all he got for his efforts was the snake's fangs through his thumb. Paul was taken to hospital and the snake was taken out of town and released.

10 In Texas, beer shampoos are out. For $50 you can bubble your pleasure in a Lone Star state salon. They'll trim your locks and give you a permanent wave by pouring chilled Perrier water on your head.

11 John Arity became something of a hero in La Crosse, Wisconsin. Like the fabled Dutch boy of old, John came to the rescue to halt the flow of suds from a beer keg when his hosts at a party found their spigot wouldn't fit a freshly opened tap hole. So, John stuck his finger in. Then he couldn't get it out. After guests drilled another hole to decant the beer into smaller containers, John was taken to the hospital where he lay on an emergency room floor while the barrel was removed from his finger.

12 Some people actually get away with this hustle for awhile: If you see them in a bar and make the mistake of saying, "Howarya?", you get kind of a pained expression and an explanation..."Not bad. But I've got a bad case of yers." If you continue to be careless and ask, "What's yers?", they'll thank you for the offer and say they'll have a beer.

13 If a woman fills a glass with beer and touches her lips to the foam, it is safe to bet that the froth will disappear more quickly than if a man does the same thing. It's the grease in the woman's lipstick that will cause such a scientific reaction.

14 Remember how mom always told you to mind your P's and Q's? The phrase dates back to the folklore of English taverns. P's were for pints and the Q's were for quarts. Minding your P's and Q's was reckoning the size and number of mugs of beer consumed by the customers.

15 "Many an old-timer laments the disappearance of this ale or that lager, and becomes nostalgic about the glories of some fondly-remembered brew, when he is really mourning the passing of his youth."

—quoted in *Brewing In Canada Newsletter,* 1965

16 This letter appeared in the *Yellowknifer* newspaper: "Daphne, my darling! Call, write, whisper, moan. Tell me your flame burns bright. Our days apart have been like an empty beer can." Passionately, Biff.

17   "The men who frequent bars
The he-men and the wrecks,
They do a lot of talking
About beer and also sex.
Now it's my observation,
In spite of all they boast of,
That between the beer and women,
Beer's what they get the most of."

—Anon.

18   Condemned killer Steven Judy was executed in
Michigan City, Indiana for the slaying of a young mother and
her three small children. Before meeting his death in the
electric chair, the convicted murderer was given a sedative
after being refused beer with his last meal of steak and
lobster tails. Asked why he was given a sedative, press
secretary Jan Powell said, "It was for medicinal reasons and
beer isn't used for medicinal reasons."

19   A journal kept on the Mayflower reveals that the
Pilgrims would have sailed further south to Virginia, instead
of landing at Plymouth Rock, had they not run out of beer.

20   Father Anselm went to West Germany's Andechs
monastery for peace and quiet and to think about his doctoral
thesis in theology. However, in January, 1986, he was
appointed manager of the monastery's thriving brewery, one
of Bavaria's top tourist attractions. More than a million
people a year visit the Benedictine monastery in the village of
Andechs. The monastery has been making beer since it was

established in 1455 on the site of the castle owned by the count of Andechs, whose family died out in the 13th century. The monastery brews about 380,000 litres of beer a year. Its most popular is a dark type called Doppelbock. Having postponed the idea of completing his thesis, Father Anselm attended courses on business management and brewing. Asked if he saw a contradiction in his religious role and that of his involvement outside the monastery, he said, "Prayer is our top priority and my job is to keep things at the monastery working so that my brothers are free to pray."

21 When the late Rene Levesque was Premier of Quebec, a story went around that a new beer was brewed in his honour, called Levesque Bleu. You drank just one bottle and 10 minutes later you'd go "Oui, Oui."

22 When William "Red" Hill Jr. emerged from the barrel in which he shot the Lower Rapids in the Niagara River, his first words were, "Somebody give me a beer."

23 Message on a t-shirt spotted in Madeira Beach, Florida: "Everyone should have something to believe in. I believe I'll have another beer."

24 "Beer can be a status symbol at a chic restaurant when it's properly merchandised." So said Gene Sage, owner of four top-rated Chicago restaurants which claimed that beer can help overall sales in the dining room if actively promoted. Normally, beer in upscale restaurants is largely relegated to the bar and promoted only at lunchtime, but Sage attracted young urban professionals to his establishments by featuring a wide variety of beer. One of his popular features was a "Turn-Around-Dinner" in which local celebrities became waiters for the evening.

25 A gorilla went into a bar and ordered a beer. The bartender was a little taken aback at having a gorilla come into his bar, let alone order a beer. He decided to serve him and placed the bottle of beer in front of the gorilla. Much to his surprise, the gorilla pulled out a $10 bill and gave it to him to pay for the beer. The bartender took it to the cash register and thought to himself, "What the heck, it's just a gorilla; he doesn't know anything." So, he took only $1 from the cash register and gave it to the gorilla for his change. The gorilla took it, didn't say a thing and proceeded to drink his beer. When he had finished, the bartender said to him, "You know, we don't get many gorillas in here." The gorilla shot back, as he left the bar, "I guess not, at nine bucks a beer!"

26 For more than 450 years, Mennonites have been fighting a quiet battle against the spread of urbanization and the influx of technology into their traditional and religious lifestyle. The town of Elmira, Ontario is in the heart of Mennonite country where the conservative Old Order and Amish branches remain unchanged in many ways from what they were a century ago. Thursday is traditionally market day for Mennonites and on that day whole families can be seen travelling to town by horse and buggy. The Elmira beer store has a hitching post attached to the side of the building. Store Manager Tim Helm said the steel horse head with rings is a community service that is well used and appreciated by the rural horse-and-buggy people. He said most Mennonites don't drink and those who do come into his store are cashing in returnable beer bottles that have been discarded along the side of the road. He added, "A few of the Mennonite farmers buy porter to feed their cattle because of the nutritious aspects derived from hops, malt, barley and yeast."

27 A man found with an open bottle of beer in his car was merely using the brew to cool off an overheated engine, a District Court judge was told in Toronto. The man's lawyer said that would be his defence when the "case" gets to trial.

28 When Glenn Balmer and Murray McCreadie approached a burning car on Toronto's Gardiner Expressway they quickly stopped their beer truck to help put out the fire — even though they didn't have a fire extinguisher. Noticing flames leaping from the hood of the car, Murray jumped onto the back of his beer truck, grabbed a case of beer and both men ran back to the small car stopped by the side of the busy expressway. After assuring the owner, Gary Merkler, that the low-alcohol content of the beer would not spread the flames or ignite a bigger fire, the two beer truck drivers poured 12 bottles of beer on the car's motor to douse the flames. After their heroic deed, Glenn commented, "We don't carry bottle openers with us. Murray had the presence of mind to pick a case of beer with twist-off caps."

29 Churchgoers were kept warm in the Lancashire village of Warrington, England, thanks to a brewery. During one particularly cold December the heating system in St. Anne's church broke down and would have cost more than 1,000 pounds to repair. In a heart-warming (or soul-warming) gesture, the owners of the brewery next door offered to pipe waste steam from their plant through the church.

30 Sign on the door of a topless bar: "Sorry, clothed until further notice."

31 When Toronto was granted an American League baseball franchise in 1977, the Toronto Blue Jays became the only team in the major leagues that didn't sell beer during baseball games, much to the disapproval of most fans. During the height of the tempest that followed, it was not unusual to see drinkers' laments appearing in the daily newspapers, like this one that appeared in the Toronto Sun: "There's nothing so mournful, so sad and so drear, as to go to a ballgame where you can't buy a beer." A dozen years later, Toronto baseball fans were enjoying their favourite beverage (in rain or shine) under the retractable roof of the 53,000-seat SkyDome stadium which is outfitted with 113 draft beer dispensing taps.

32 It wasn't until 1982 that the Premier of Ontario announced that the sale of beer at Blue Jay baseball games at Toronto's Exhibition Stadium would be permitted. However, Hon. Larry Grossman, the government's consumer minister at the time was against the idea, saying he didn't want some drunk sitting behind him in the stands "puking" on his kids. Despite his objections, chugging suds at the ballpark became part of the game in Toronto. In 1987, Gretchen Drummie of the *Toronto Sun* wrote a story about ballpark beer. The article began, "It's been five years and nobody's puked on Larry Grossman's kids during a Blue Jays game."

33 At Vermont ski resorts, beer has always been an integral aspect of the active "apres ski" scene but it was also part of the PRE-ski scene one year. Skiers who brought in

100 empty beer cans or non-returnable bottles could exchange them for a one-day ski ticket at the Mt. Vernon ski resort. The program was part of a Vermont 'clean-up' day one spring.

34 Swigging beer, meditating, wolfing down lasagna, avoiding sensual pleasures and even running are some of the ways entrants in the Boston Marathon prepare on the day before the world's most famous foot race. On Sunday, April 16, 1978, before the 82nd marathon, the 2nd annual carbohydrate-loading party was held at Eliot's, the famous runners' pub around the corner from the finish line at the Prudential Centre. Most of the world's top long distance runners were there, where Tommy Leonard "the running bartender" presided over a calorie-loaded feast featuring spaghetti with three different kinds of sauces and plenty of beer. "Beer is good for you in moderation," said Tommy.

35 Cross-country skier Eric Shine wandered for four days — lost, hungry and cold — often having hallucinations in the trackless snows of the California High Sierra. In a hospital bedside interview in San Francisco, following his harrowing ordeal, he told an incredible story of existing on leaves and acorns, losing his ski poles, breaking his ski bindings, fearing for his life and digging out snow caves in which to sleep. On the fourth day of his tribulation, he awoke determined to get a grip on himself. To his everlasting relief, he discovered at a stream the first sign of civilization he'd seen in several days — discarded beer cans.

36 Ever since the first beer can came on the scene in 1935, as many as 12,000 different styles of beer labels have been produced in the United States. One of the fastest growing hobbies is the collecting of breweriana such as empty beer containers. Now, each year, thousands of members of the Beer Can Collectors of America attend beer can CANventions around the country.

37 Bill Rogers, of Melrose, Mass., won the 82nd Boston Marathon in 2 hours, 10 minutes, 13 seconds; finished all the press interviews on the winner's platform, showered and got dressed by the time Keith Durham completed the 26-mile, 385-yard course. Durham, an ambulance supervisor from Uxbridge, Ontario, struggled over the finish line in 3 hours, 14 minutes to the cheers of thousands of spectators. "All I want now is a beer," he said with a grin. Keith took up running a few years prior to the 82nd Boston Marathon to try and get rid of his beer belly.

38 To avoid potential dehydration, runner Jim McDonough once reportedly drank 36 bottles of beer the night before the qualifying race in the Pan-American Games. He qualified while many others dropped out, thus creating a legend and a standard that may not be equaled.

39 A motor boat called Hangover won the 3rd Annual Cup Beer Can Regatta in Darwin, Australia. Hangover was made from 4,000 beer cans. Fifty craft, made from almost 250,000 beer cans took part in the eight-race program. Nearly 15,000 people watched the races. The boats, all shapes and sizes — including Spanish galleons, paddle steamers and barges — were required to rely on beer cans for 90 per cent of their flotation. Powered by a 135-horsepower outboard engine, Hangover easily won the five-lap world cup event around the 250-yard course at an average speed of 25 miles-per-hour.

40 When Don Cherry was coach of the Boston Bruins National Hockey League team, he was a favourite among the media pundits who specialized in the jock talk trade. Here's what Cherry said about his best friend Whitey Smith: "He's not a hockey fan, which really gets me. Him and I are just good drinking buddies. He drinks rum and I drink beer. I forgive him for that."

41 When Don Cherry made it to the big time as a National Hockey League coach, he said he was just as happy coaching in the minor leagues. "I drank as much beer. I had a nice car. I didn't have as nice suits as I do now and it was draft beer in those days". When asked if he was a drinker of imported beer, Cherry replied, "No, just Budweiser. That's my beer, just Bud."

42   Former Montreal Canadien hockey star Henri Richard once took part in a blind beer taste-test. The owner of a Montreal tavern, Richard was a self-proclaimed Molson Export drinker. He took part in the test, sponsored by the *Montreal Gazette* newspaper, with a panel of seven other people. For sampling, the panelists tasted unmarked glasses of Molson Export, Laurentide, Labatt's 50, Labatt's Blue, O'Keefe, Carlsberg, and Heineken. Richard correctly named only two — Laurentide and Heineken. "I'm not too proud of myself," he said. "I must have had too much last night."

43   North American sportswriters didn't give Leon Spinks much of a chance in defeating World Heavyweight Boxing Champion Muhammad Ali prior to the pair's bout so many Februarys ago. Obviously, the sporting world hadn't realized that the future champ had been conducting sparring sessions during his training period with Oliver Phillips, a six-foot-five-inch Las Vegas beer truck jockey.

44   In front of Crazy Art's Beer Emporium in Myrtle Beach, South Carolina, "Bullett" Bob Oldham used to give demonstrations of what he did best. Mr. Oldham was adept at opening beer bottles with his eyebrows.

45   Forest Golden was intent on having all non-returnable containers banned in the United States. So, he drove from his home in Auburn, N.Y. to the Vermont Legislature to testify in favour of legislation to ban non-returnables. Mr. Golden drove his point across by completely covering his vehicle with empty beer and pop cans.

46 In its search for the perfect beer mug, one U.S. brewer tried to outshine all the others by introducing, as a point-of-sale item, a glass with a snap-on base, containing a battery and a bulb. The beer glass gave new meaning to the term "light" beer.

47 In its search for the perfect beer glass, a brewery in London, England, introduced a goblet-shaped glass with a round stein and a slightly nipped-in top. It was said to have all the qualities to get beer into the mouth and not down the shirt.

48 The Kalevala, the national epic of Finland, describes the creation of the world in 200 verses but it takes 400 verses to describe the origins of beer.

49 You don't have to attend medical school to become a doktor. Each year, thousands of people throughout the country receive Beer Doktor awards at Oktoberfest celebrations in such places as Frankenmeuth, Michigan; Kitchener, Ontario; and Munich, Germany. A Beer Doktor Award is presented to anyone who can drink a "humpen" (23.5 ounces) of beer without taking their lips from the glass.

50 To publicize the opening of a nightclub in Hamburg, Germany, a public relations firm came up with a promotional idea right off the top of their heads. They invited all of the city's barbers to a special party. Within a month the new club was booming. The talkative barbers, as expected, had told all their customers about the evening.

51 A drink of beer was part of the act when the Falcons, a British army paratroop team, took to the air. Newspapers around the world carried a picture taken by Flight Sergeant Terance Allen who photographed Sergeant Brian Sulton serving a glass of beer to Sergeant Tony Charlton while both men were heading for ground zero with their parachutes still unopened.

52 The patron saint of beer is Saint Gambrinus.

53 Billy Carter, the late brother of former U.S. President Jimmy Carter, had a beer named after him. In recognition of the "Billy Beer" honor, he said, "For me the beer thing was a natural, 'cause I know a good beer better than anybody. Who knows? Maybe I'll become the Colonel Sanders of beer." Following Billy's death in 1988, an ad appeared in a New York newspaper, advertising six-packs of Billy Beer for the incredible sum of $9,000 each!

54 "They who drink beer will think beer."

> —The Sketch Book, Stratford
> Washington Irving
> 1783-1859

55 Theatre owner Martin Shafer always had two criteria for judging movies—how they did at the box office and how they did at the bar. When Shafer ran two movie houses in Dearborn, Michigan and nearby Westland, he sold alcoholic drinks and allowed patrons to take them to their seats. He said he had no problems with people drinking too much beer "because people don't come to the movies to drink, they come to watch the show." He added, somewhat wistfully, "Now, if I could get a desert picture like Lawrence of Arabia, I'd have it made!"

56   "I think of all I miss
The boys I used to know;
The girls I used to kiss;
The coin I used to blow;
The bars I used to haunt;
The racket and the row;
The beers I didn't want;
I wish I had them now."

      —Robert Service
       The Telegraph Operator

57   The owner of a Fort Lauderdale laundromat took the drudgery out of doing the wash by selling beer and wine. He added another twist when the "suds" were flowing, topless dancers. The Helpy-Selfy Laundromat didn't have a cover charge but the cost of draft beer went up 35 cents a glass while the show was on.

58   It was a Friday night at 8:45 p.m., the busiest time of the week, and Bob Hodge was working at the cash counter of a Toronto beer store when it happened. Thirty male customers were in the store when Bob looked up and noticed the lady in front of him was stark naked. He later recalled, "She ran across the front of the store and butted in front of the line. She asked for a case of beer and plunked her money on the counter. I just stood there dumbfounded." The naked lady said, "Well, aren't you going to get my beer?" Bob called out the brand and waited for the case of beer to be sent down the roller from the refrigerated area situated at the rear — that is, the back — of the store. "I didn't answer her," said Bob. "I just stared at the change and counted it VERY slowly. When the case of beer came down the roller, the woman grabbed it, ran out the door and hopped into a waiting taxi." Following the incident, Bob was asked if he could identify the lady. He said he didn't notice the colour of her eyes but estimated she was about five-feet, six-inches and very hefty. "Before she came in, there was the usual chatter and noise from the customers," Bob reported. "But during the time she was in the store there wasn't a sound. You could hear a pin drop. But as she was leaving, all of the customers started clapping and cheering."

59 In Thornwood, New York, a beer distributing firm and Carling's New York Sales Division made a display out of 12-ounce cans of Black Label beer. They stacked 7,056 cases to create a record-breaking display that amounted to 2,032,128 fluid ounces of beer.

60 Motorists in Victoria, British Columbia, were able to run their cars on empty beer bottles for awhile. Gulf Oil dealer Derick Stratford swapped 50 cents worth of gasoline for a dozen empties. He said he decided to do something positive about cleaning up parks and roadways that were littered wih beer bottles. When he first started trading gas for empties he was receiving up to 500 bottles a week.

61 George Hall reported seeing a case of Old Vienna beer on a picnic table in Forest, Ontario. The picnic table was perched on top of a sloped roof of a house. George said, "In Mount Forest, they drink beer in funny places."

62   There was once a western Canadian maverick brewer everyone called Uncle Ben Ginter. The late brewer's company, Uncle Ben's Industries in Richmond, British Columbia, once accepted worthless bottle caps that could be traded in for worthless stock in the company. Two hundred used bottle caps would be accepted in return for 10 shares of the company. The program, announced by Uncle Ben himself, would permit 30,000 shareholders in Manitoba, 50,000 in Alberta and 91,800 in British Columbia. The shares had no value, but the new shareholders could have representative directors on the company's board.

63   Five men in Melbourne, Australia, were convicted in court of stealing a ton of beer every week for nine years. That's 720 bottles every week...37,440 a year...more than a third of a million bottles in nine years. One of the men was a beer delivery driver who admitted stealing from his employer.

64 When a spokesperson for a brewery in Sudbury, Ontario was informed that thieves had smashed their way into his brewery and walked away with four dozen bottles of his product, Northern Ale, he said, "They have good taste."

65 The Adolph Coors Company and its local distributor in Jacksonville, Florida filed a civil lawsuit in September, 1988, alleging fraud against a construction worker who claimed he found a dead mouse in a 16-ounce can of Coors beer. The suit claimed that James Harvey attempted to steal money from the brewery through deception, fraud and deceit after he asked the company to pay him $50,000. After the case hit the headlines, it was discovered that James Harvey had been involved in a May, 1988 traffic accident with a tractor-trailer owned by Coors. He was not injured but his car was totalled. Coors won the fraud case when it was proved that the mouse-in-the-beer case didn't hold water.

66 An illustration of a wide-eyed and majestic moose, stamped on the labels of Moosehead beer, has been the symbol of this Canadian Maritime product for many decades. Derek Oland, President of Moosehead Breweries in Nova Scotia, explained the symbol this way: "What that moose means is good Canadian beer — clean water, clear skies, green grass, woods, hunting, fishing, all that." But in 1988, 60 years after the first case of Moosehead pale ale rolled off the line, the brewery launched new packaging for its Moosehead pale ale. Mark Tunney, writing in the Saint John Telegraph-Journal, noted that a new "designer" moose now peers out from a traditional background. Tunney quoted Philip Oland, Chairman of Moosehead Breweries Ltd. as saying, "They call it a sleeping moose, but sometimes I think he almost looks dead."

67   "On the breasts of a barmaid from Quaile
Were tatooed the prices of ale
While on her behind
For the sake of the blind
The prices were tatooed in braille.

     —beery limerick published in *Froth Talk*
     a newsletter of Creemore Springs Brewery.

68   "The nice thing about buying beer is that no one ever asks what year you want."

     —Quoted by Irene Sax in Long Island,
     N.Y., *Newsday*

69   The bikini-clad models on the bottles of Nude Beer can't take it all off in Arkansas. The state's beverage control director, Robert Moore, said the labels violate a state regulation that prohibits "any coupon or other inducement to purchase an alcoholic beverage." Mr. Moore said the federal government approved the labels because the models are clothed at the time of purchase. But, he noted, the latex labels can be scraped off with a thumbnail.

70   When professional food and beer photographer George Biss pours a beer into a glass, he does so with the tenderness of a portrait artist, the finesse of a surgeon and the skill of a sculptor. He said he has never used shaving cream to get a whiter head of beer, saying, "People are demanding a more natural look, so it's not necessary to use phony tricks to make the product look more appealing." He and his son, Greg, admitted they "spritz" the outside of a glass of beer before taking a picture because a major food and beer shoot might take all day and it's obvious that a one-inch head on a glass of beer isn't going to last long under the glare of studio lights. Some photographers use a mixture of water and glycerine which they spray on the glass to create the long-lasting droplets of water on the outside, giving it a cool, refreshing appearance for a longer period of time. Others use water and syrup. George and Greg wouldn't divulge their secret ingredient for competitive reasons. The father and son team said they sometimes go all day without eating. "When you're shooting food or beer, you don't think about eating or drinking it," said George.

71 Many U.S. brewers are involved in nation-wide alcohol-education programs to teach young adults and others the dangers of alcohol abuse. One that received a lot of attention was an ad by Adolph Coors and Company. The brewery collaborated with movie producer Steven Spielberg to create a poster for bars and restaurants in which E.T. admonishes, "If you go beyond your limit, please don't drive. Phone home."

72 As part of a campaign to encourage the moderate consumption of beer to fitness-conscious individuals, the Pabst Brewing Company developed an advertisement known as "best-beer-bellies-in-America." The ad for a low-calorie beer showed the firm midriffs of bathing beauties and gymnasts. There was not a beer drinker's paunch in sight.

73 The President of Stroh Brewery Co. admitted that beer and the methods of advertising the product were more severely criticized in the mid-1980s than at any time in his life. "We feel we have to find a way to present the good side of alcohol," he said. "Before we're through, we may come to the conclusion that beer is better for you than breakfast."

74 Michael Farber said Canada is the worst drinking country in the world. In his newspaper column, the *Montreal Gazette* writer lambasted everything related to drinking in the country—from the mindless advertising to "depressing ambiance." He referred to Montreal taverns as having "all the charm of abandoned airplane hangers." He dismissed the popular French brasseries (pubs) as taverns with hanging plants or hanging hockey sticks. In contrast, he noted that beer in Belgium is served with the care normally given to vintage Dom Perignon.

75 It is no longer wimpy to order a light beer. So said Gregory Dollarhyde when he was Vice-President of TGI Fridays, operators of more than 100 of the popular drinking spots in the U.S. "There's a reverse psychology at work," he said. "You're going to be fat and unattractive if you don't [order it]. Image is very key."

76 Drinking light beer is all a part of self-love said Gene Street. Speaking as principal owner of SRO, a fashionable Dallas restaurant and bar that featured full-length mirrors in the men's lounge, he added, "There's no such thing as a fat yuppie."

77 A little-known artifact, found in the Smithsonian Institution, is a booklet called *Toasts*, published by the Wm.

J. Lemp Brewing Company of St. Louis, Mo. Discovered in the Warshaw Collection, the booklet contains numerous toasts, including this one by George Arnold:

"Here, with my beer, I sit; while golden moments flit;
Alas! They pass...unheeded by.
And as they fly, I being dry,
sit, idly sipping here, my beer."

And this one by W.L. Hassoldt:

"None so deaf as those who will not hear.
None so blind as those who will not see.
But I'll wager none so deaf nor blind that he
Sees not, nor hears me say, 'Come drink this beer!'"

78 One of the longest running stage plays in Quebec theatre history was *Brew*. The show exposed a day in the life of a tavern—the Chez Willy—situated in the heart of Montreal. In one scene, a customer at the Chez Willy is feeling faint so it is suggested that he hold two cold bottles of beer under each armpit to prevent him from passing out. A tough-looking motorcycle gang member enters the tavern and approaches the wimpish customer who has the protruding beer bottles peeking out from each armpit. "What are you?" asks the tough guy, "A vending machine?"

79 In days of old, the British used a rather unique method of beer quality control. An inspector, called an "ale conner," spilled a little beer on a bench and sat on it while quaffing a pint of the new brew. If, after a while, it stuck to his leather breeches, it was determined there was too much sugar in the beer and was, therefore, impure. The entire batch of beer would then be poured down the drain.

80 W.H. Brooke wrote a rather unique magazine article entitled "What'll We Drink To In March?" Just as it sounds, Brooke's item listed 31 beery items which we can celebrate on any given day in March. Pick a day...any day..okay, March 26th. Here's what Brooke suggested we do on that day: "Have a tall frosty one for inventor William Painter. If it weren't for him, you'd still be battling with a cork every time you opened a bottle of beer. Painter invented the crown cap for bottles and the 'church key' opener."

81 On January 1, 1915, the good people of Iceland voted to ban alcoholic drinks. The ban was partially lifted after Spain refused to buy Iceland's main export, fish, unless Iceland bought Spanish wines, and in 1933 prohibition was repealed — except for beer. But in May, 1988, Iceland's parliament voted to legalize beer after a 73-year drought. Following a year-long debate, a full turn-out of the upper house voted 13-8 to stamp out the last vestiges of prohibition on the island and permit the sale of beer with an alcoholic content above 2.25 per cent, beginning March 1, 1989.

82 The 5th annual Great American Beer Festival, which was to be held in Denver in the summer of 1986, was postponed due to "the present insurance climate." Disappointed organizers explained that since a rash of legislation limiting liability was passed in several states, no liquor liability insurance policies were being written in Denver until the status of the law was clarified. At the previous domestic beer festival, 94 beers from 50 breweries were displayed and tasted.

83 Consumption of beer was disallowed aboard a Millardair DC-3 which the New Democratic Party of Ontario had rented to transport party officers and members of the press during the province's election campaign of 1977. The reason for the dry runs was that beer was being blamed for incessant trips to the aircraft's lavatory which resulted in too many plumbing problems. One pundit termed the official explanation "verbal diarrhea."

84 Relations between the media and certain politicians reached a new low during a particular Ontario election campaign when the Liberal Party began charging for the beer on the press bus. It didn't take reporters very long to realize that they were paying more than the cost of the beer. Not wanting to be accused of contributing to the party's treasure chest, members of the media did the only honourable thing. They began to bring their own beer on board.

85 By 1981, the care and coddling of the news media at election time in Ontario was of prime concern. The policy, as outlined by the three political parties and reported by Rosemary Speirs in the Toronto Star on February 4, 1981, was as follows: "The Conservative Party agreed to serve sandwiches and beer on tour. The Liberals would provide snacks and beer but would expect reporters to pay for the beer. The New Democratic Party had no plans to serve anything, but officials said the bus would stop to pick up beer on the way home."

86 In the future, not all brewery products will be cold and foamy. According to a research newsletter from the

University of Wisconsin, we could be chewing goods produced by brewers. A brewery by-product — spent brewers' grain — has been used as a flour replacement to create high fibre cookies. The grain serves as a nutritious substitute for about 15 per cent of the flour in a normal commercial recipe for chocolate chip, oatmeal, molasses, ginger, peanut butter and sugar cookies, with no noticeable taste change.

87 Anyone who doesn't believe the Soviet Union takes its booze seriously ought to have a little chat with Galina Nikitina. If they can find her. Miss Nikitina was Chief Barmaid at the Plysain Cafe in Moscow's central Gorky Park when it was discovered she'd been watering down the beer in her establishment. She got 15 years for her crime. It was reported that she and seven co-conspirators had been selling the diluted beer at premium prices. One of her shady colleagues got nine years in a labour camp and the other six were sentenced to eight years apiece.

88 In Hildenborough, England, a judge sympathized with motorist David Starkey who lost his taste for beer as the result of a crash. "I regard that as a great loss," the judge said and awarded him $14,076 in damages.

89 The makers of de-alcoholized beer are fighting hard to find a niche of their own. "Buzzless brew", as it is called, is considered to be a large "untapped" market but it's got to be good, said Tom Voss, a spokesman for Australia's Swan Special Light. Insisting that the public will drink very low alcohol alternatives if it tastes good, Voss added, "As my father used to say, you can't kid the goldfish by feeding it sawdust."

90 It wasn't easy for some of the spectators to watch a huge bulldozer crunch 1,077 cases of perfectly good beer at the city dump in Rifle, Colorado. "It's the saddest thing I've seen in the Roaring Fork Valley since Sheriff [Bob] Hart had to burn 1,000 pounds of marijuana," one man said at the scene. The beer was smoke-damaged in a fire at a Glenwood Springs warehouse. The contents of the cans and bottles were not damaged in the blaze but the manufacturers refused to allow the tarnished containers to be sold.

91 Not everyone is excited about the proliferation of new beer, such as dry beer, red beer, seasonal beer and pale ale. Whatever happened to plain and simple, good old beer? Before light beer came on the market, the brewers' attitude was: "If God wanted us to brew a different beer, Granddaddy would have done it," said Robert Weinberg, professor of marketing at Washington University and a former executive of Anheuser-Busch Co. Despite the popularity of dry beer and draft, brand proliferation will continue, predicted Emanuel Goldman, of Paine-Webber Inc., of San Francisco. But, said Goldman, in the *Wall Street Journal,* there are only so many varities on a theme. "Now you've got Bud Dry, you aren't going to get barbecue-flavoured Bud Dry."

92 On a hot, July day in Windsor, across the river from Detroit, the outdoor temperature sign in front of a meat packing firm read 85 degrees Fahrenheit. At the same time, down the street about one mile, the Labatt's brewery sign indicated the mercury was at 92 degrees Fahrenheit. One local scribe suggested that perhaps the companies wanted to let the public know that it wasn't too hot to cook meat for dinner but it was plenty hot enough to drink beer.

93 A variation of this dog-eared joke appeared in *Suds 'n Stuff,* a California-based newsletter for members of Beer Drinkers International: "One day in a bar in the Wild West, a dog walks in, goes up to the bar and says, 'I want a beer.' The bartender replies, 'We don't serve dogs here.' The dog answers, 'I've got money and I want a beer...now!' A customer pulls a gun on the dog and says, 'He told you he don't serve dogs! Now get out before I shoot you!' Just then the gun goes off and the dog is hit by the bullet in the left leg. Blood pours out as the dog limps to the door. About six months later, the dog returns to the bar, but this time he is dressed in black, with two six-shooters on his hips and a cigarette hanging out of his mouth. The bartender recognizes him and says, 'I told you before...we don't serve dogs here!' The dog replies, 'I don't want a drink. I'm looking for the man who shot my paw!'"

94   Sister Doris Engelhard, a member of the Poor Franciscan Order, once beat out 26 men to gain her master brewers diploma in Mallersdorf, West Germany. With assistance from another nun, she was able to brew about 3,300 pints of beer annually from barley grown on the convent farm. The light-colored beer brewed at the Mallersdorf convent was sold locally and had an alcohol content of 12.6 per cent. On special occasions, like Christmas and Easter, Sister Doris marketed a stronger brew containing 16 to 18 per cent alcohol.

95   A saloon bar in Britain, in the Bridge House Hotel, once installed a time clock and distributed time cards to regular male patrons who were ordered to check in and out. The saloon manager said he was fed up with irate wives who would telephone and refuse to believe that their husbands had just left. About 50 of the married customers agreed they too were tired of begging their wives to believe they had only been at the pub with the boys. "We have got to be united over this," the manager said. Anyone failing to clock in and out had to pay a six-pence fine to a local charity.

96   A High Court judge in London, England, once ruled that a wife may divorce her husband if he spends every night at his local pub.

97   Beer has been the basic beverage of mankind from the beginning of recorded history. One of the earliest documents known to man is a clay tablet inscribed in Babylonia around 6000 B.C. which depicts the preparation of beer. By 4000 B.C., the Babylonians were making 16 types of beer from barley, wheat and honey.

98 In the 1930s, a beer brewed in Hamilton, Ontario, was best known for its slogan: "Spell it backwards." The name of the beer was Regal.

99 In the movie *Deliverance*, Burt Reynolds was seen drinking a can of Lucky Lager Beer.

100 One of the world's most famous beer slogans was coined by the Jos. Schlitz Brewing Company when it decreed that theirs was "The Beer That Made Milwaukee Famous." That one phrase, which has become a part of American folklore history and an icon among world beer legendary slogans, has spawned shaggy dog stories like this one: A baseball pitcher by the name of Milt Famey was told he wouldn't be called upon to pitch in a particular game, so he sat in the dugout and had a beer. It was a hot day at the park, and since he wouldn't be pitching he decided to have another beer while watching the game. Then he had another one. And another. The game was a cliff-hanger that went into the last inning with the score tied. By the bottom of the 9th, Milt's manager had gone through his entire pitching staff and had no choice but to send his now-mellow pitcher into the game. Milt slowly made his way to the mound and proceeded to walk the first batter he faced. He also walked the second batter. He threw four pitches to the next player at the plate — all balls. When he walked the fourth batter, the winning run crossed the plate. After the game, several players from the winning team strolled past their opponent's dugout. One pointed to the many beer cans strewn on the ground and declared, "That's the beer that made Milt Famey walk us!"

101 The once-popular T.V. series *Laverne and Shirley* was set in Milwaukee, one of the world's beer capitals, but that didn't seem to impress the show's two female stars. Penny Marshall told an interviewer she doesn't drink beer. "It makes me go to the bathroom," she said. Her co-star, Cindy Williams, was even more forthright, "I hate beer. It gives me gas." One T.V. critic responded to Cindy's remark in this manner: "Gee, that's precisely the same reaction I get watching *Laverne and Shirley.*"

102 "There's nothing — well practically nothing — as good, on God's green earth, as a cold beer." These words were uttered by actor Paul Newman as he snapped open a can of beer while being interviewed many years ago in the back of a rented Cadillac limousine as it headed for an airport. Newspaper columnist George Anthony was seated with Newman and the movie star offered him an ice-cold beer. Later, Anthony reported to his readers that Newman "ordered another beer upon entering the airport's first-class lounge and boarded the plane, mentally ordering his next beer in advance."

103 Paul Newman was once asked about the circumstances surrounding his departure from Ohio's Kenyon College back in 1949. Newman quipped, "I graduated magna cum lager."

104 This could only happen in Hollywood. The script of a particular movie (now long-forgotten) called for a bottle of Schlitz beer. However, the bottle of beer was missing from the set. A studio car and driver was sent to a nearby market. The driver's time was charged against the production as was the car's rental time. The production was also charged overhead for the driver and the car and there was interest on the overhead. The final cost of the bottle of Schlitz was $300.

105 Country music singer Tom T. Hall once expressed his sentiments about beer: "Well, I really like beer. After my wife has ordered a gourmet meal in a nice restaurant somewhere, I ask for a bottle of beer. I've had to explain to her hundreds of times it's just that I like beer. After it happened again one time, she said I should write a song about it. So I did." Tom's big hit single "I Like Beer" was at the top of country music's popularity charts for 15 weeks after it was recorded.

106 Pancho, a 30-year-old burro that was drinking 30 quarts of beer a day, was ordered to cut down his drinking by veterinarians who said he had a liver problem. The Cuban news agency "Prensa Latina" reported in April, 1989, that Pancho—famous throughout the island—must stop entertaining customers by drinking beer in a bar near Holguin in eastern Cuba. Pancho would be put out to pasture but wouldn't have to go on the wagon, the agency said. Aware that withdrawal might be bad for Pancho, veterinarians allowed him 10 quarts a day. Pancho began drinking 15 years ago when a patron gave him a bottle of beer and he delighted customers by braying for more. Patrons have been buying him drinks ever since.

107 Geronimo is—make that "was"—the world's biggest land snail at eleven inches. When it died in London, its owner denied that a switch from a beer diet was a contributing factor. Chris Hudson said, "He was six years old and he just died of natural causes." The giant snail gained fame in nightclubs with its ability to guzzle beer in the same fashion as its late mother, nicknamed Boozy. But the Royal Society for the Prevention of Cruelty to Animals put its foot down and Hudson was forced to put his snail on milk instead. Hudson, a breeder of snails, said Geronimo weighed 1.3 pounds and grew four inches in one year. The snail's shell was put on display at the Natural History Museum.

108 In the 1960s, when William Holden was a 60-year old movie star, he went to a California slimming spa because he was a "heavyweight and a heavy drinker." According to Dr. Philip Smith, author and medical director at the time at La Costa, a spa for the rich and famous in Carlsbad, California, seven thousand people were said to have lost one million pounds in 13 years. Dr. Smith reportedly told Holden to switch from hard booze to beer. The doctor later reported that Holden got off liquor altogether and at 160 pounds was about seven pounds underweight.

109 She has settled down to become a wife and mother now but when Caroline Kennedy was younger, her mother, Jackie, worked hard to cultivate her daughter's palate and prepare her for a life of sophistication. As a 21-year-old, however, it was reported that Caroline preferred sausage pizza over quenelles de sole au gratin and would take a beer (swigged from a can) over vintage champagne.

110 Chip Carter, the son of former U.S. President Jimmy Carter, said his father never drank Billy Beer, the brew endorsed and named after the brother of the former head of state. Chip said his father didn't drink beer because of an allergy to hops.

111 An Australian court ruled in favour of bus driver John Francis who claimed that he was entitled to collect three free mugs of beer a day, for the rest of his life, from a local pub. The Captain James Cook pub, in the Canberra suburb of Narabundah, was ordered by a judge to honour a raffle prize, which Francis won, for the free beer. The tavern had paid up for five years after the raffle, but when the hotel chain sold the establishment, the new owner was unwilling to give the beer away. A thirsty Francis appealed to the courts. "I've got at least 37 years of beer drinking left in me," an exultant Francis said after the decision was handed down in his favour. He calculated he could drink 40,000 mugs of free beer before he died.

112 The manager of Britain's smallest pub quit because he couldn't get enough people inside to make it worthwhile, and it was driving him nuts. Ted McMullan managed the tiny drinking spot which measured seven feet by fifteen feet. The landmark puny pub was appropriately named The Nutshell.

113 A beer stein owned by William Schwartz, of Lancaster, Pa., was carved from the tusk of an elephant shot by former U.S. President Teddy Roosevelt, in 1908.

114 One of the largest beer steins in the world was modelled by A.J. Ger in 1820. The colourful tankard is 46.8 inches high, weighs 35.3 pounds empty and can hold 8.5 gallons (U.S.) of beer. The ornamental work, which took 15 months to complete, was produced from the well-known Brueghel painting *Flemish Country Wedding*.

115 The Canadian Press news agency reported in May, 1989, that the residents of Vernon, in British Columbia's Okanagan Valley, might have a beer-loving monster on its hands. Ogopogo—the area's answer to the Loch Ness monster—is depicted as a beer-snatching monster. Even though its existence has never been proven, it is usually portrayed as an affable creature. (Vernon holds a copyright on the use of the monster's name and depiction.) Local city council wasn't impressed when they first heard that a beer company had decided to turn the creature into a beer-snatcher for a commercial. But after watching a preview of Ogopogo involved in a tug-of-war for a six-pack, they enthusiastically endorsed it.

116 The romantic legend of Viking warriors, as portrayed in movies and comic books, is that they were beer-chugging, horn-helmeted macho men who plundered and pillaged villages in a savage manner. In truth, these seafarers of 1050 A.D. wore plain, hornless helmets and usually drank water or sour milk. These mainly peaceful craftsmen, peasants and merchants reserved their beer drinking occasions to special festivities.

117 Jim Anderson of Houston, Texas, went on a $3,000 shopping spree and ended up with a pair of used bloomers. Not just any bloomers, mind you. The ones he bought were once worn by Queen Victoria. Mr. Anderson outbid two others at an auction at Fort Langley and the bloomers, which once warmed the royal bottom, were soon hanging behind the bar of Jim's English-style pub in Houston.

118 The late "beer baron" E.P. Taylor once flubbed his lines in a speech he was giving about horse racing and betting. In his pitch for off-track betting, the industrialist and financier spoke of the loss of revenue to "bootleggers...er, bootmakers...ah, bookmakers!" As the crowd in the room began to twitter, Taylor came back with a quick retort: "I used to be in the beer business," he explained. Taylor had owned Canadian Breweries Limited, Canada's largest brewery at one time.

119 A newspaper photo appeared in the late 1970s showing the reclusive Greta Garbo. The information under

the picture stated enigmatically: "Staying alive with beer."
The caption added that the former actress "dances the nights
away in Swiss resorts and discos and drinks beer.

120 A person-in-the-street interview, by *The Toronto Sun*
during a heat wave, asked people how they keep cool in hot
weather. A woman said she tucks up her dress at her belt and
lets the breeze blow when the sun gets a little too hot. One
man said, "I put a cold beer between my belt and tummy. It
takes about three minutes before my whole body is cool."

121 Mr. Anthon W. Nielson was known as one of the
world leaders in the brewing industry when he was director of
United Brewing of Copenhagen. His home was in the Danish
brewery's huge Carlsberg compound and his passport listed
that address. Once, when passing through the immigration
area of an international airport the immigration officer
studied Nielson's passport and stated, "No one lives in a
brewery." The brewery executive responded: "Excuse me, but
the Pope lives in the Vatican and I live in a brewery." The
officer sort of bowed his head and motioned with his hand as
he intoned, "Pass through, friend."

122 Hamper MacBee was a notable moonshiner in the
heavily-wooded mountaintop area of Monteagle, East
Tennessee. He once waxed philosophic, "I took a drink of
water recently and I want to tell you something. Water is okay
to bathe in or shave in but as a beverage it's a 100% failure."

123 When Captain Shingi Ishida brought his skyjacked
Japan Airlines 707 back to Tokyo, he was met at the airport

by his two daughters who greeted him with two cold bottles of beer.

124 Pauline McGibbon is a gracious and grand lady who once served in the official capacity as the representative of Queen Elizabeth II in Ontario, Canada. On one particular occasion, Lieutenant Governor McGibbon was photographed sipping a beer with some university students. Upon seeing the newspaper photo, many citizens got their shorts in a knot and complained about the vice-regal representative drinking beer in public. One letter to the editor suggested the lady wasn't a lady. The *Sarnia Observer* newspaper put the critics in their place with an editorial that said, in part: "True to form, she [the Lt. Gov.] has ignored the trappings of tradition and has done something she felt like doing because she is a person. Bravo, Pauline, and may the dark robes of ceremony continue to fall by the wayside."

125 When a Canadian government official once announced that the government was considering watering down draft beer from an alcohol volume of 5% to 3%, the pronouncement earned this diatribe from Scarborough construction worker Kenny McCoombs: "They can up my rent a few bucks. They can charge me more at the supermarket because that's a fact of life these days. But God help them if they try anything with my draft beer. When I kiss goodbye to the job, I just want to lap up that good old, ice-cold draft. Just let 'em try and water it...just let 'em try." The government plan was subsequently dropped.

126 City officials in Moscow approved plans to open 133 new bars, automatic dispensers and restaurants to sell beer as part of a more balanced approach to Mikhail Gorbachev's anti-alcohol campaign. But the *Moscow News* said in a 1988 article that Muscovites still have to be lucky to find a bottle of beer anywhere. Moscow city officials also ordered a 19% increase in beer production in 1988, but *Moscow News* said breweries cannot meet their deliveries because of a shortage of bottles.

127 Beer drinkers and litterbugs the world over may be justified in claiming the "Margaret Fuller incident" as their finest hour. Margaret Fuller was a passenger on the 34,000-ton cruise ship Windsor Castle. At 8 a.m. on August 6, 1976, the 64-year-old woman fell overboard while the ship was sailing toward Cape Town at 12 knots. Her plunge into the drink was not noticed for about an hour, at which time the ship turned around and tried to retrace its path, apparently not an easy task for a vessel of this size. Luckily, however, passengers aboard the ocean liner had been tossing beer cans overboard for the last hour and Captain Patrick St. Quentin Beadon followed the floating cans back to Mrs. Fuller who was pulled safely from the water. Her husband later said, "It was a miracle that she was saved and I only thank the officers and crew for their good work." He didn't mention the passengers and their beer cans.

128 Robert H. Uihlein Jr., the late chairman and chief executive officer of the Jos. Schlitz Brewing Company, was well-known for his witty, off-the-cuff remarks. In 1965, 70,000 people attended a Schlitz-sponsored concert featuring the New York Philharmonic Orchestra in Central Park. One observer questioned whether the brewery's investment in fine music helped to sell Schlitz beer, and pointed out to Mr. Uihlein that at the opening night concert, empty beer cans of other brewers were strewn on the ground but there were no Schlitz cans. Uihlein responded, "Schlitz drinkers are quality drinkers. They use receptacles for their beer cans."

129 We're not sure who came up with this blooming idea but why don't the environmental people ask the brewers of the world to design a beer can that will look pretty as a wild flower beside the road?

130 Henry Koch is most probably the man responsible for getting beer in cans sold in Ontario. It seems that a few decades ago, the Business Editor of the Kitchener-Waterloo Record wondered why the province's breweries were allowed to package beer in cans for export markets but not for Ontario. The Editor called the government minister in charge of liquor regulations at the time, Allan Grossman, and asked about it. Grossman told him that if the breweries wanted to market canned beer in Ontario, they'd get a favourable reception from his department. "The breweries asked and that's how we got canned beer in Ontario," said Koch, who added, "I still don't know if I did mankind a favour."

131 At a seminar in Chicago, a business communicators group was told that a scarcity of aluminum in the United States was causing delays and higher costs in the construction of missiles and aircraft. A conference attendee facetiously suggested that the shortage arose because "they're using too much of the stuff for beer cans."

132 The oldest brewery in the world is the Weihenstephan Brewery in Freising, near Munich, West Germany, founded in 1040.

133 The oldest brewing company in North America is Molson Breweries, founded in 1786, in Montreal, by John Molson.

134 The art of tasting beer is known as organoleptics.

135 Most professional beer tasters pour beer into a glass with a one-to-two-inch head of foam. They smell the beer through the foam and then take short sniffs after swirling the liquid when the foam has subsided. The many flavour and taste sensations experienced by the palate is described either verbally or in writing. There are four basic taste sensations that are experienced on a particular area of the tongue. They are: salty (tip of the tongue); sweet (tip of the tongue); sour (side of the tongue); bitter (back of the tongue).

136 Plans to give breath tests to drinkers at a farm show in the town of Malvern, England, were scuppered by a brief beer strike. Farmers at the Three Counties Show had been invited to blow into a new Japanese-made alcohol meter before leaving the grounds so they would know if they were fit to drive home. A strike at a nearby brewery halted deliveries to the three-day show. However, the strike was settled before the show ended and hundreds of farmers and visitors enjoyed the local brew and took the breath test as they left the grounds. "I do not know of any farmer who considered himself unfit to drive," an official said.

137 When it was first reported that beer was being used to test diamonds in Sierra Leone, British gemologists received the information with a great deal of mistrust. But after testing the claim, they found it to be true. Diamonds and spinels immersed in beer reflect the light in a characteristic manner, thus proving their authenticity. So, don't be surprised next time you see a woman dunk her ring finger into a glass of beer. She's merely testing the integrity of the man who gave her the rock.

138 A British company once marketed a plastic, air-tight bag containing six, one-quarter litre packs of light ale. The new container required less shelf space than conventional bottles and seemed easier to store in the refrigerator. The bags were tested in London, but consumers found the beer bags to be "messy." Also, technical problems by the manufacturing company proved difficult to overcome.

139 An American scientist, Dr. Ole Sandven, gave the world this food for thought: "The time may be coming when a person may be able to pour a cool drink from a bottle and then, for a snack, munch on the bottle itself."

140 A proposed law aimed at standardizing beer production in Germany was nixed soon after it was suggested. Germans protested that the suggested all-European law, which was being worked out at the European Common Market Headquarters in Brussels, would pollute their national drink. When a brewery expert from Bonn told a group of West German legislators that the law would permit glucose, sulphur dioxide, ascorbic acid and proteolytic enzyme to be added to beer, the government body cried"boo!" in unison. The nation's breweries took out full-page newspaper ads calling on drinkers to protest the law.

141 "The House of 101 Beers" in the town of Starnburg, 15 miles from Munich, once boasted that it featured the world's largest collection of "unusual beers" from 24 countries. Actually, there were about 135 different beers. When the proprietor of the Bavarian inn was asked, several years ago, why he carried beers from China, Africa, Iceland and Australia but none from the United States, he replied that American beers, because of the chemical content, didn't pass Germany's strict brewing laws which go back to the year 1516. Some of the more unusual beers at the quaint inn were oyster beer from Ireland and a smoked beer from Poland that had a ham-like flavour. One beer, from Kulmbach, claimed an alcohol content of 28% and another came in an odd-shaped bottle with a printed serial number on it. It was sealed with a thick circle of red wax and came from a brewery in Treuchtlingen, founded in 1516. Reportedly, they mature the beer for several years in special temperature-controlled cellars before sending it to market.

142 Throughout its history, beer has been known by such endearing names as huff-cap, stingo, and Pharaoh.

143 In the Czechoslovakia town of Satb, the hop harvest has always been a time of celebration for the townspeople.

Locally-brewed beer flows freely during the festival and everybody joins in the dancing in the town's main square. One novelty dance has the male dancer holding his partner in his arms and balancing a tankard full of foaming ale on his head. The dancer with the last tankard to survive the balancing act wins the annual contest.

144 Out of some 80,000 pictorial stamps issued around the world during the past few decades, only a handful depict the brewing industry. Most "beer stamps" are found in Europe and in one country in particular — Czechoslovakia — the home of Pilsen beer. The country has long considered the brewing industry important enough to be featured on stamps and often shows hops and hops harvesting as an important source of local employment. One stamp, issued in 1956 to publicize natural resources, depicts a woman gathering hops while another 1961 stamp pictures hops and a glass of beer. Yet another is the 1 Koruna value stamp showing an ancient view of the city of Pilsen and a bottle of Pilsen beer.

145 Margaret Winfield was chosen Britain's "ideal barmaid" nearly two decades ago when she won the title over 3,000 contestants. Margaret was picked for the honour partly because of her talents in pulling a pig's ear, serving a dog's nose, a mother-in-law, a granny, a wallop and a wompo. A pig's ear is the cockney term for beer. A dog's nose is gin with a beer chaser. A mother-in-law is a mixture of stout and bitter beer and a granny is a mixture of "old and mild beer." Wallop and wompo are kinds of ales.

146 "Ale shoulder" has joined the list of traditional occupational hazards of tennis elbow and housekeeper's knees. A London doctor was baffled when a busty woman visited his office complaining of upper-chest pains. She told Dr. Steve Cembrowitz that she worked as a barmaid in a pub that dispensed pints of beer through an old-style hand pump instead of a gas-powered tap. Writing in *World Medicine,* Dr. Cembrowitz noted that "the consequent increase in muscular activity of the shoulder...resulted in chronic strain of the shoulder fibres."

147 When it was declared unlawful in the United States to have bars exclusively for men, some male-oriented establishments found ways to discourage women from entering their preserve. Charles W. Merritt, former President of the American Hotel and Motel Association, told a group of hotel owners about a well-known bar in New York that was successful in discouraging women. "Whenever a man entered with a woman," he explained, "all the men would stand up and start applauding and keep it up until she left. Eventually, women just stopped going there." Another observer suggested that some previously all-male establishments returned to being all-male "because women found the places, and the men they found there, not very interesting."

148 In August, 1974, Beverly Sutherland caused quite a stir when she entered the men's beverage room at Toronto's Skyline Hotel and ordered a draft beer. Mrs. Sutherland had stepped into what was considered to be a male preserve, so her request for a beer was ignored. That was at 4 p.m. Nearly five hours later—after a waiter served a man at Mrs. Sutherland's table and following a 10-minute wait while the waiter consulted his superiors—a beer was brought to the lady-in-waiting. Having made her point, she left. Here's what one 15-year veteran patron of the room had to say about the "intrusion" of a woman in his male domain: "Maybe women got their rights. I figure we got our rights too. That's all. The working man made this hotel. So now, if they let women in here, let's face it, what the hell are we guys gonna do?"

149 When a Quebec government working group first recommended in the 1970's that taverns for men-only should be eliminated, the air was blue in Quebec City taverns, like the Taverne Royale, for instance. Here's what two of the male patrons had to say: "They've got their hairdressers, why can't we have our taverns?" "It's the last male sanctuary."

150 A famous English bar, frequented by journalists from London's Fleet Street, was well-known for its steadfast refusal to serve women at the bar. The rule was once tested by a man dressed in women's clothing who revealed his gender in no uncertain terms after being refused service. Without a moment's hesitation, the bartender said, in that case, he would have to wear a tie in order to be served.

151 The late newspaper columnist Dennis Braithwaite, who was often tagged as a "crusty curmudgeon," had this to say in 1970 when he was writing for the now-defunct *Toronto Telegram*: "The men's beverage room is the only castle left to the ordinary Canadian citizen-slob. To take it from him is unnatural, unnecessary, unwarranted and cruel."

152 A tavern-owners' convention in New Orleans once featured the editor-in-chief and publisher of a feminist magazine as the main speaker. The female publishing executive presented information on what women expect in a tavern. Prior to hearing her speech, one tavern owner said he was surprised that the topic was even being discussed. "I was under the impression that women expect to find beer and men in a tavern."

153 In Ireland, pubs are a focal point — a meeting place — and at last count (in 1989) there were 10,000 pubs in the land. In the Irish capital of Dublin there are more than 850 pubs spread throughout the city. Writer Patricia Tunison Preston notes that it was in *Ulysses* that James Joyce referred to the puzzle of trying to cross Dublin without passing a pub, but then he abandoned the quest as impossible, preferring instead to sample a few in his path.

154 A champion marksman in Britain said the secret of his trophy-winning skills was attributed to his consumption of 30 pints of beer a day. The 56-year-old marksman admitted that was his regular intake when he scooped top prizes at the famous Bisley shoot in the 1960's. He claimed the beer helped him hit parts of the target that other marksmen could not reach, by tightening his eyeballs to make him see better. A spokesman for the man's favourite brewery said, "Our beer is by no means weak. Anyone who drank 30 pints of it in a day would have great difficulty seeing anything — let alone a target!"

155 After drinking six pints of lager, a motorist in Kent, England, was stopped by police and ordered to take a breath test. The driver passed the test but he was none too happy about it. He later wrote an angry letter to his local consumer protection office claiming that the beer he'd consumed was understrength. The complaint was checked out but tests showed that the brew in question was indeed up to par.

156 A carload of nuns was spotted driving along a city street in England sporting a sign on the car's rear bumper which warned: "Don't drive if you're drinking. There's no cure for the mourning after."

157 Two Yorkshire men were paid to go on an extended pub crawl. Stephen Crook and Peter Cressy were financed by a TV company to seriously research British drinking habits. Said Crook before embarking on the dream assignment, "We will have to keep our heads fairly clear in order to watch other drinkers."

158 Former British Prime Minister Harold Wilson once fought the battle of the bulge by drinking beer. His personal belt-tightening program in the mid-1970's resulted in the loss of eleven pounds from his somewhat chunky frame. At a luncheon in Manchester one day, he attributed the weight loss to a ration of four pints of brew a day. "Contrary to all medical opinion, I've lost a lot of weight since I began drinking more beer," he told the gathering. The PM explained that he had stopped drinking hard liquor after deciding to drink more beer. "I certainly feel better now that I've turned to beer," he said. "By golly, it's doing me good."

159 Lager was only "discovered" by the British a quarter of a century ago. Prior to that time, a pint of bitter had been an Englishman's favourite drink and only one pint in 100 sold was a lager. The Chairman of the Brewers' Society said it was not until the "swinging 60's" that lager really caught on in his country. "People holidaying abroad, particularly in Germany and Austria, found it a nice, clean, refreshing drink and started asking for lager back home."

160 Ken Crietchlow hitch-hiked his way around the world in 97 days dressed in a pin-stripe suit and a bowler hat—all for a pint of beer. He bet he could do the trip with only 10 pounds sterling. He came back to his north London home with money to spare.

161 *Advertising Age* magazine once reported the results of a survey that showed wives made more decisions than their husbands when it came to choosing food and beverages, with two notable exceptions: beer and wine. The U.S. survey, which measured husband/wife influences on buying decisions, showed that although 41% of wives buy beer, 79% of the brand choices are made by men.

162 Many an Irishman has sworn on his dead mother's soul that the single factor distinguishing Dublin Guinness from its overseas brands is the waters of the Liffey. In fact, Guinness stout of Ireland is made from the limestone waters of St. James Well in County Kildare, 30 miles southwest of Dublin and not from the waters of the Liffey. The brackish, grey ooze that slowly moves past the brewery in Dublin is the Liffey.

163 Jimmy Robertson was a beer slinger in the Winchester Hotel beverage room on Toronto's Parliament Street, and in 43 years of serving suds in the same room he was never late for work and always wore the beverage room waiter's traditional dark pants and white shirt. Jimmy retired in 1977 at the age of 77. He was earning $3.10 an hour when he left. Bar room brawls were not uncommon in the area where he worked, but Jimmy usually played the role of peacemaker. "I only got involved in one big one and that was when two young guys started picking on an older fella," he said. Jimmy and his wife, Barbara Ann, left Canada to retire to the Orkney Islands north of Scotland where they'd purchased a small house in the tiny village of Holm, overlooking the North Sea. "I once promised my mother that I'd come back home some day and I guess that's what I'm doing," he said shortly before he retired. "My mom and dad are gone now, but I still feel something for the old land."

164 Guinness Brewery was one of 216 breweries in Ireland in 1832. Now it's one of the largest in Western Europe but only one of a few left in Ireland.

165 Billy Porter was once the chief of publicity at Guinness headquarters in Dublin. He said the word "stout" originally was an adjective to describe an extra strength porter.

166 A survey taken several years ago by a business magazine called Vision, revealed that the people of Ireland are Europe's biggest drinkers — of milk. The survey showed that the Irish drink an average of 47 gallons of the white stuff every year. The next most popular beverage is beer, at 24 gallons per head.

167 A recipe for the brewing of Hekit, a beverage made from water and barley fermented by crumbs of bread, was chipped on a clay tablet 6,000 years before the birth of Christ.

168 The Pharaohs sipped beer while pondering plans to build the pyramids.

169 There is at least one job that will never be performed by a machine. The task of organolepticology (beer tasting) is safe, according to a research physiologist who said no laboratory can replace human taste buds. Speaking at a technical session at a Master Brewers of America convention, he explained his thesis, "Beer makes its impact on many senses: taste, smell, touch, temperature, muscle sense, hearing and vision. Of these, the most significant is smell. Although there are thousands of taste cells, there are millions of odour receptors. While playing a secondary role to odour, taste is still critical for flavour. For this and other reasons, the human subject must remain the ultimate arbitrator of beer qualities."

170 In 1876, when Louis Pasteur discovered the process
that bears his name, for killing bacteria, he was more
concerned about beer than milk. Commissioned by brewers,
Pasteur was experimenting with methods of protecting yeast
when he hit upon his theory of "pasteurization."

171 On a day in October, 1969, a small group of brewery
workers walked off their jobs for about an hour. The
disgruntled workers at Formosa Springs Brewery, north of
Toronto, returned to work after the brief disruption when
management said there had been a misunderstanding and
assured them that a wage increase, promised for October 1,
would be coming. It was the first walkout at the brewery in
more than 100 years.

172 Police were called in to control traffic in Darwin,
Australia, when a mile-long line-up of thirsty people formed
soon after a liquor store announced it had 1,000 cartons of
beer for sale. Darwin's brewery workers had been on strike
for a month when the store offered its bonanza stock for sale.
The 1,000 cartons, selling at $12 each, were gone in 29
minutes.

173 It's not often that a newspaper will endorse a
commercial product but that's exactly what an editorial did in
the Kirkland Lake, Ontario, *Northern Daily News* in 1978.
Readers were told they could make an important contribution
to the economy of Northern Ontario by drinking one of
several brands of beer produced by Doran's Breweries which
had plants in four Northern Ontario cities. The company was
in its 2nd year of employee ownership. (Of 175 employees,

85% had elected to buy into the company when shares were offered.) The editorial writer stated that "every ounce of Doran's beer that succeeds in making its way through Northern Ontarian lips has a direct effect on the local economy."

174 When Wilmat Tennyson was president of Carling O'Keefe Breweries he was once asked to donate money toward a bike-a-thon organized by a charity organization in Toronto. He refused to give them money, but offered his sweat. "It's easy to give money but it's tough to give sweat," said the then 40-year-old executive who promised to ride 60 miles at the bike-a-thon and obtain pledges for each mile covered. When word of his participation got around, pledges poured into his office. Following the event, he was able to donate more than $5,000 to the Variety Club's work in helping handicapped youngsters.

175 In the early 1960's, naval tradition suffered a blow by the Duke of Edinburgh when the Prince refused the traditional tot of rum when he visited the British guided missile ship *London*. "No," said Prince Philip. "I cannot abide rum." And he had a glass of beer instead.

176 It would appear that 1974 was a good year for beer. For the first time in its 125-year history, the Jos. Schlitz Brewing Company reached the billion dollar mark in sales. The total was $1,015,978,000.

177 "Anheuser-Busch has a juggernaut going now," said Jerry Steinman, publisher of the *Beer Marketer's Insights* newsletter. He made the comment after the world's largest brewery announced that its sales jumped 5.2% in 1987 and its share of the lucrative U.S. beer market rose to nearly 40%. The company sold 76.1 million barrels of beer that year.

178 Beer is still the king of alcoholic beverages, according to a Gallup poll in the fall of 1987 that revealed little change in the drinking habits of Americans over the past few years. Of the 65% who said they drink, 50% said they drink beer most often.

179 Beer seems to slake the thirst of stranded people when nature lavishes floods upon its helpless victims. One spring, in Caledonia, Ontario, the waters of the Grand River rose to record levels and flooded many homes, leaving homeowners completely and helplessly surrounded by water. A photo that was published in newspapers around the country, showed a group of rescue workers in a boat, handing supplies to a woman on the doorstep of her partially-submerged house. The picture clearly showed the grateful woman accepting a case of beer from her good samaritan friends.

180 Graham Kerr, best known as TV's Galloping Gourmet, claimed that when he was about to go into the British Army his father decided to take him out and get him drunk. "You know the thing," Kerr explained. "'You're about to become a man, my son' and all that. A quaint mid-Victorian custom. Well, he was drinking scotch and I was drinking beer and after awhile he was nearly paralytic, but I was still drinking beer."

181 The cattle township of Hall's Creek, Australia was once isolated for four months as the result of monsoon rains. Soon after the small town of 500 was cut off from the outside world a telegram was sent to the Darwin supplier from the town's only storekeeper: "Please air freight — as many as possible — cartons of canned beer in place of usual perishables. Desperate. Town out of beer." Food on the next plane into Hall's Creek was replaced by 100 dozen cans of beer. The telegram orders, in the following weeks, read as follows: "Operation beer highly successful. Desperate again. Can you repeat this week, plus four bags potatoes, one bag onions." "Town still thirsty. Require more beer this week." "Require beer, milk, ice cream, six bags potatoes, one bag onions." "Need ice cream, milk, potatoes, onions, and as much beer as you can load!"

182 Japan placed 4th in beer production in the world in 1987. World beer production increased by 3.2%, and China boosted its production by a whopping 30.5%. Japan's largest beer maker, the Kirwin Brewery Co., said it was expanding its beer production and would surpass Britain's in 1988.

183 Moosehead beer, brewed in the Canadian Maritimes, was the 4th most popular of nearly 400 brands imported into the United States in 1987.

184 For nearly 30 years, Budweiser, "The King of Beers," has reigned supreme over the $16 billion beer industry in the U.S. The brand accounts for one of every four beers consumed in the nation, according to the *Wall Street Journal*, October, 1988.

185 "Life ain't all beer and skittles, and more's the pity; but what's the odds, so long as you're happy."

    —"Trilby," pt. 1
       George Louis Palmel la Busson Du Maurier
       1834-1896

186 "I'm only a beer teetotaler, not a champagne teetotaler."

    —"Candida," Act III
       George Bernard Shaw
       1856-1950

187 A house built in 1910 and situated in the Saskatchewan town of Goodwater was completely covered with beer bottles to serve as insulation. The job of applying the bottles was undertaken in 1965 by Ralph Grenville who was 79-years-old at the time. It took him an entire year to collect the bottles and place them on the house—very carefully.

188 A rather unusual bridge was constructed in a city in Michigan. It was a 20-foot-high model of the Marquette County Harbour Bridge and it was made out of beer cans (the model, that is). The structure contained 18,000 beer cans and it stretched 100 feet in length and measured 100 feet wide. The bridge was built by a group of university engineering students. Who else?

189 At Polytechnic Institute in New York, beer cans were used in an event called Beer Can Racing. Entrants from engineering schools (where else?) were allowed to soup up their cans any way they wanted, without altering the shape. The winner was a Miller beer can with a soldered flywheel inside. Second place went to a Carling can with a rubber band and a pendulum.

190 A man in Bisbee, Arizona, was hoping to ride a tide of empty beer cans into the White House, a number of years ago. As a declared "candidate" for the presidency of the United States on the United American Party ticket, he had planned to finance his campaign around the country by collecting beer cans along the highway and turning them in for 15 cents a pound. The man, his wife, seven children and family dog were able to collect only 250 cans along the highways. They carted them halfway across the state of Texas to a brewery only to discover that the cans were made of steel, not recyclable at the time and therefore, worthless.

191 For years, some Canadians expressed consternation over certain provincial laws that forbade the sale of alcoholic beverages during polling hours on the day of an election. During one particular federal election, one drinker said he refused to vote because, "If I can't think, I can't vote and I can't think if I can't drink." Another opinion came from Basilidas Kwok who suggested that what the country needed was a good beer-flavoured ice cream on election days.

192 Don Wright, a one-time corporate communicator, commented on Canadian agriculture figures in the following manner: "These (statistics) show that more than 2.77 million tons of grain were used during the last three years for the manufacture of beer and liquor. The rest was probably wasted."

193 Canada's chief delegate on the Vietnam peace-keeping force in the early 1970's, Michael Gauvin, told of the morning he was invited to breakfast with a member of the Viet Cong's Provisional Revolutionary government. "I asked for fried eggs, sunny-side up," Gauvin said. "But there was a great deal of difficulty in interpreting the words 'sunny-side up.' In the end, they gave me a beer."

194 During Buffalo's infamous bone-chilling, butt-freezing winter-of-'77 snow blizzards, there were a few stories of price gouging by local merchants. At one suburban hotel, beer was priced sky-high but a stranded customer reluctantly paid the greedy innkeeper, saying, "What are ya gonna do? We weren't gonna spend the whole night cooped up in that place with no beer."

195 A Polish gentleman, Mr. Jreneusz Chrominski, wrote the following letter from Warsaw to a Canadian beer company: "KOLEKCJONUJE NALEPKI OD. PIWA. NIE POSIADAM JESZCZE NIC Z TEJ FIRMY. PROSITBYM O PRZSTANIE ZA CO Z GORY DZIEKUJE." A batch of Canadian beer bottle labels was immediately sent to Mr. Chrominsky, a beer label collector, as requested.

196 The average West German downed 146.6 litres of beer in 1987. (That's 38.7 U.S. gallons.) East Germans were 2nd in the world in terms of per capita consumption at 140 litres (37 gallons.) Third place went to Czechoslovakia and fourth to Denmark. Americans drank 90.8 litres (24 gallons) and the average Canadian downed 81.87 litres (21.6 gallons).

197 A man of dubious character and questionable intelligence entered a Las Vegas bar and yelled to the waiter, "Gimme a beer." The waiter replied, "We don't serve riff raff in here." "That's okay," the man answered. "What other brands do you have?"

198 Then there was the guy who moved into a friend's house and brought seven pieces of luggage — a six-pack and a can opener.

199 Did you hear about the guy who filled his waterbed with beer because he wanted a foam mattress?

200 A fellow was told that someone by the name of Sexbreak worked for a Milwaukee brewery. Half believing the story, the guy called the brewery and asked: "Do you have a Sexbreak there?" The receptionist replied, "Are you kidding? We don't even get a coffee break!"

201 The Reverend John Joyce, of Hildersham, England always believed that a man's public house is the pub and God's public house is the church. The good reverend liked a pint of beer now and then and figured his parishoners should enjoy the same pleasures. That's why he had a notice posted in his church recommending his favourite pub and a sign in his favourite pub advertising his church. "This joint venture," he said, "will help strengthen the link between man's public house and God's public house."

202 When the Quebec Tavernkeepers' Association agreed to raise the price of draft beer by 10 cents a glass, sales in Quebec taverns dropped drastically. The president of the association said he received more than 100 calls from panicky tavern owners who reported poor sales. The president was quoted as saying, in what could only be described as a plaintive whimper, "I think we made a mistake."

203 "The British stand up sometimes for a woman but always for a beer. It's a question of respect," a French visitor to England discovered some time ago. "Foreigners are fascinated by that strange custom of drinking while standing up. Everywhere else in the world, other than in a British pub, the patrons sit down while they drink." Describing the scene at an annual Brewers' Exhibition, he reported, "It is all very earnest, but then, beer is an earnest drink. Beer is always just beer — solid and reliable as an English oak."

204 The Cronmiller and White Brewery no longer exists in the Welland-Port Colborne region of western Ontario but there are a few oldtimers who remember the oft-quoted slogan: "I'll have a little more Cronmiller and a little less White." Translated, that folksy saying of a bygone era meant: "I'll have a little more beer and a little less foam."

205 Following the publication of a lengthy and extensive study of alcoholic beverages a number of years ago, an official of the Association of Canadian Distillers was asked for his comments and views on the report. "It's a lot of twaddle," he said.

206 Trevor Lautens once commented in the *Vancouver Sun* about the "coming out of beer" from smoky saloons to snotty salons. Here's what he had to say: "Personally, I doubt if I can handle the new beer snobbery. I, an honest working-class boy, could scarcely suppress the giggles when sniffing wine corks in obedience to the democratization of vinous snobbery that began [a few decades ago]. Sometimes I had to shove a cork up my nostril to keep from snorting altogether. Damned if, while a female and a waiter expectantly look on, I am going to start sniffing beer caps."

207 In the days before Mikhail Gorbachev's glasnost (openness) and perestroika (restructuring) policies, some Soviet Union party officials decided that the best way to counter drunkenness in the country was to close down beer halls throughout the land. One Soviet enemy of beer wrote the following tirade: "Systematic beer-drinkers get an enlarged heart and bad circulation. The veins get thicker, twisted and knotted. The real boozer gets a bulbous nose and bad complexion, runs to fat and looks disgusting."

208 One of the most eloquent tributes to beer appeared in the now-defunct *Liberty Magazine* and was penned by the eminent newspaperman, H.L Mencken, who wrote: "My regard for malt liquors amounts to veneration, and I fear that if I let myself go on the subject I'd bust into dithyrambs and maybe into tears. Beer belongs to the end of the day. It begins to be good as the sun goes down and it goes on increasing in virtue until the sandman makes his rounds. It is the perfect drink for the shank of the evening...it harmonizes perfectly with all the light and pleasant trifles of the table — sandwiches, bread and cheese, crackers and so on. It can bear communion with salads...it slakes the thirst, shuses the medulla oblongata, warms the stomach, and fans the imagination. More good music has been written on beer than all the other drinks of mankind put together. There is little risk of slipping an overdose of it, for it is transformed into blood, bone, hair, and ideas almost as fast as one can get it down."

209 E.J. Pyler also wrote often in praise of beer in his role as Editor and Publisher of *Brewers Digest*. Here's one of his editorials in honour of the virtues of good old-fashioned beer: "It is difficult to place much faith in the self-appointed diviners of American taste preferences according to whom the public can barely restrain its thirst for new and alien flavours in their beers—flavours that are guaranteed to revive presumed jaded appetites and impart new impetus to lagging beer sales. What this approach ignores is the fact that beer, brewed with care according to classical traditions, remains among Nature's truly noble gifts to mankind. The willful tampering with its innate quality in an attempt to alter it to suit some imaginary flavour predilection on the public has met with failure in the past, and there is little cause to believe that it will succeed in the future."

210 Not all of the silver-tongued venerations of beer are as elegant as the previous epistles. Some are more, shall we say, unadulterated and earthy, containing within themselves a somewhat basic purity of not only the drink itself but also that of the language as well, such as the comment by Graham Hughes, of Etobicoke, Ontario, who once articulated his opinion of outdoor pubs: "They're great. You can work on your sun tan while you sock back the suds."

211 The following classified ad was placed in the "Births" column of a Victoria, B.C., newspaper, by Richard and Jane Trench. At the time, Richard was Brewhouse Supervisor at Labatt's Brewery in Victoria,"TRENCH; brewing supervisors, Richard and Jane, are pleased to announce that after eight-and-one-half months in storage tank, the new brew was finally ready for bottling on February 22 under the label of Cara Marnelle, 7 lbs. 8 oz., joining happy half-pint Lisa at home."

212 If you find yourself in any one of the following 34 lands, you won't go thirsty if you know how to call for a beer in the correct way. Here's how to say it best in more than 30 languages:

ALBANIA	Bierre
BELGIUM	Biere
BULGARIA	Bira
CHINA	Mai chiu
CZECHOSLOVAKIA	Pivo
DENMARK	Ol
ENGLAND	A pint
FRANCE	Biere
FINLAND	Olutta
GERMANY	Bier

GREECE	Bira
HOLLAND	Bier
HUNGARY	Sor
ICELAND	Ol
INDIA (Hindu)	Biyar
ITALY	Bir
INDONESIA	Birra
IRELAND	A ball of malt
ISRAEL	Bior
JAPAN	Biou
LATVIA	Alus
LITHUANIA	Alus
NORWAY	Ol
PHILLIPINES	Serbesa
PORTUGAL	Arveja
POLAND	Piwo
RUSSIA	Pivo
SERBIA	Pivo
SOUTH AFRICA (Afrikaans)	Bier
SOUTH AFRICA (Zulu, Afrikaans)	Vbhiya
SOUTH AFRICA (Zulu, Kaffir)	Utchwala
SPAIN	Cerveza
SWEDEN	Ol
TURKEY	Bira

213 In 1983, Alfred "Freddie" Heineken and his chauffeur went through a three-week kidnap ordeal. Both were released unharmed after a ransom of $11 million was reportedly paid (later most of it was recovered and several people arrested). The Dutch beer baron helped Heineken Breweries grow from a domestic supplier to a worldwide concern after he joined the firm in 1942. The firm was founded by his grandfather. Alfred Heineken planned to retire as chairman when he reached the age of 65 in 1989.

214 Eighty per cent of Canadians drink alcohol according to a 1988 Gallop poll. Use of beer, liquor or wine is highest among Canadians aged 18 to 29 at 86 %.

215 There was a time when the Liquor Licence Board of Ontario ordered a ban on the public display of posters advertising a beer festival because the word "beer" appeared in the ad. Organizers of the 1970 Kitchener-Waterloo Oktoberfest were told by the Licence Board that a beer licence would not be issued for the festival unless the offending word was removed from the literature promoting "Canada's Great Beer Festival." The organizers followed the letter of the law and got their licence. New advertising posters announced that "Special Bavarian Milk" would be served. Some people started calling Oktoberfest the "Great Canadian Barley Juice Festival" and others promoted the sale of "lemonade with a froth."

216 In the 1860's in Augusta Township, near Brockville, Ontario, there were so many breweries in the area that farmers often received free pails of beer on hot summer days. All they had to do was spread the good word about a particular brewer's product. It is an early example of "word of mouth" advertising.

217 An Ortlieb Brewing Company TV commercial that denounced light beer once won honours from the Brewers' Association of America. In the days before light beer became a heavyweight in the marketplace, the ad featured Joseph W. Ortlieb commenting on the low alcohol beers. The commercial began with an announcer saying, "Joe Ortlieb almost announces Ortlieb's Light Beer." Then, Joe, himself, is shown dropping two ice cubes into a half-full glass of Ortlieb's beer, saying, "Plop, plop, fizz, fizz to make a light beer. That's why I don't. I make beer for people who don't take their taste lightly." The announcer wound up the commercial with this folksy suggestion: "Try Joe's Beer. Ortlieb."

218 Pubs in Britain and Wales no longer have to close for two-and-one-half hours every afternoon as they've been forced to do for the past 71 years. In 1988, the House of Commons scrapped a rule that had been part of the country's fabric for more than seven decades and no longer do patrons have to hurriedly gulp that last pint of ale each afternoon when bartenders bellowed "last orders." Patrick Brown, assistant manager at the Red Lion in the West End of London welcomed the rule change, saying it would "do away with your mad afternoon rush and business will be spread over the afternoon."

219 A woman in Lowbanks, Ontario, created a Beer Egg Nog recipe which she claimed, makes the bust grow. You'd think she'd take a patent out on this one but since she hasn't, here it is: "Mix in a blender three tablespoons of fruit sugar, with two egg yolks, until fluffy. Add one bottle of beer, mix it again, then drink it."

220 And then there's the drink that calls for two scoops of vanilla ice cream to one bottle of beer, then mix. This concoction is called, "Moby's Dick".

221 "Strip and Go Naked" is the name of this sexy beer-mixed drink: Pour one small can of pink lemonade into a pitcher. Fill the lemonade can with gin and add to the lemonade. Add a full bottle of chilled lager beer, stir, then pour into a tall glass and garnish with lemon slices.

222 The royal family of the Czars of Russia were known to be connoisseurs in the art of tasteful habits, and one of their habits, so the story goes, was creating exotic drinks such as Beer Moskovsky, Punch Moscowette and Moscory. The latter is made from 2 oz. rye, 1 oz. lemon juice, garnish with lemon and orange slice in a pilsner glass filled with beer. The Moscory can also have 1 oz. of vodka added and mulled with a hot poker.

223 Geoffrey R. Fanaken of Willowdale, Ontario, created a beer recipe and had it published in the Brewers Retail magazine, *Kegs & Cases*. Geoffrey's recipe for "Cowbeer" is as follows: One bottle of light beer, one can sweetened condensed milk, nutmeg. Fill about two inches of a triangular-shaped pilsner glass with condensed milk. Slowly pour the beer on top of the milk. Stir slowly with a spoon until well mixed. Sprinkle a bit of nutmeg on top. "It's lovely, smooth, thick and rich," said Geoffrey.

224 If you like your beer in bulk, there's something called Portage du Fort Punch. Bert Charlebois published the recipe in the *Ottawa Citizen*: 24 pints of beer, ale or stout, 80 ounces of tomato juice, 1 dozen fresh eggs, half teaspoon salt, half teaspoon pepper, 3 ounces lemon juice. Beat the eggs and lemon juice then stir into the punch. Top the mixture with a few sprinkles of grated cheese.

225 A pot roast called Beef 'n Brew was the winning recipe in a *McCall's Magazine* cooking contest, one year. The recipe, which was picked from more than 21,000 entries, included 16 ounces of beer in the cooking ingredients and suggested beer or wine as the accompanying beverage.

226 Most connoisseurs of man's oldest and favourite beverage are familiar with the most basic of beer-mixed drinks such as Bloody Lager, Beer Shandy, Beer Collins, Pink Paradise and Lime 'n Lager. But there are many little-known beer-related drinks, like Florida Slosh, Spoaty Yoaty, Clamabeer, Grannie's Special and Sneaky Pete. The latter concoction is said to be "smooth as silk and will melt the hide off a buffalo."

227 Genovese Camlin celebrated her 94th birthday in February, 1978, by tearing up her $8,200 tab at a Greenwich Village bar in New York where she had downed at least one bottle of Guinness stout daily for about 10 years. "She was 83 when she asked if she could run up a tab," said saloon-keeper Danny Lettieri. "And I figured, how long could it last?" The tavern was open seven days a week so Miss Camlin was able to drop in every day for her Guinness, which was like a vitamin pill to her, according to Lettieri. Miss Camlin was known to visit the No Name Bar every day after lunch. The bar was located only half-a-block from the nursing home in which she lived. In later years, she had upped her intake to two bottles a day, followed by a martini. Lettieri said allowing Miss Camlin to tear up her bill was the least he could do.

228 A glass of beer can cause hot flushes in some drinkers and send them into sneezing fits, according to a London laboratory report. Dome Laboratories said those stricken in this way have an allergy to the yeast in beer and the only cure is to stop drinking it.

229 Utah bureaucrats once passed a bill ordering liquor outlet owners to advertise "upfront" a warning to imbibers about the hazards of drinking. However, state officials were frothing mad when some owners took the edict literally by imprinting the law on t-shirts and distributing them to barmaids. A shapely and healthy-looking Chris Collins posed for photographers in her t-shirt at a Salt Lake City hotel. The message on her chest read: "WARNING: The consumption of alcoholic beverages in this establishment may be hazardous to your health and the safety of others." One customer said his wife told him if he kept on reading the warning, it could very well become hazardous to his health and safety.

230 A team of medical men from Guy's hospital in London, England, conducted a 1960's experiment with young healthy teeth by soaking the bicuspids in 14 different solutions for six weeks. Results of the survey showed that teeth soaked in fruit juices developed cavities. Those soaked in beer were as good as new.

231 During Prohibition, in the 1920's, Canadians could only purchase alcohol from a pharmacist to treat such maladies as apoplexy. Humourist Stephen Leacock remembered visiting drug stores during that dark period in the country's history and seeing "apoplexy cases lined six deep."

232 In the 1970's, in Brandon, Manitoba, a pharmacist once filled a prescription calling for a dozen bottles of beer. The Manitoba Medical Service allowed this one-time only prescription for "medicinal use," for an 86-year-old woman who was prescribed 12 bottles of beer—a one-month supply. The provincial medical body paid for the beer as well as the prescription charge.

233 A story on the increase in teenage drinking appeared in *Chatelaine Magazine* a number of years ago, in which the author suggested that teenagers tend to drink the way their parents do. Writer Catharine Sinclair asked an official of the Addiction Research Foundation for his suggestions on "safe drinking." His first tip? "Teach a preference for beer and wine over spirits."

234 Another vote of preference for the beer beverage industry once came from Anne Wanstall, Food Editor of the *Mirror Newspaper* in North Toronto. Miss Wanstall said beer is the healthiest of all alcoholic beverages.

235 A convention of the American Medical Association was once told that beer is a safe substitute for water and other liquids that can cause illness among travellers. A doctor from the New York Hospital-Cornell Medical Centre said, "There is no bad beer produced anywhere in the world [because] the field is too competetive." Another doctor said beer is one of the best things to prevent dehydration "because you get the salt." Another medical expert warned, "Drink it out of the bottle; don't pour it into a glass which might be dirty." A final bit of good news for beer drinkers came from Col. James Burke, who was with the Walter Reed Medical Centre in Washington, when he pronounced, "Beer does another good thing. It keeps your kidneys open."

236 Women who have a bottle of beer, a glass of wine or a mixed drink every day reduce their risk of getting heart disease and stroke by as much as 50%, according to a medical study published in the summer of 1988. Previous studies have shown that moderate drinking lowers the risk of heart disease in men but little was known about its effects on women until the study was reported in The New England Journal of Medicine.

237 Beer is an appetite stimulant high in potassium, low in sodium and has a diuretic effect, according to Dr. Dwight Peretz, clinical professor of medicine and cardiology at the University of British Columbia. At a 1987 conference on family medicine, he noted that as consumption of alcohol increases, so does the level of HDL cholesterol—the so-called good cholesterol—which carries fats from the blood to the tissues. He said drinking a moderate amount of beer, wine or other liquor daily seems to have a positive effect on the heart.

238 A group of senior citizens was told by a doctor that alcohol, taken in small quantities, could add to a person's lifespan. Dr. Lawrence Power, representing Wayne State University in Michigan, told the group of elderly people that a bottle of beer a day would never hurt them. He said,"The problem is that some people don't drink beer by the bottle, they drink it by the case."

239   In his book, *The Gourmet Guide To Beer,* author Howard Hillman explodes many myths about beer, like the legend that large bubbles are a sign of quality beer. (Just the opposite is true.) Hillman has this to say to beer drinkers who insist that beer should be poured down the side, not the middle of the glass: "Don't be shy about pouring a fair-sized head; that's what the brewer intended you to do. If you don't release some of the excess carbonation, too much of the gas may end up in your stomach. Exceptions to the down-the-middle rule are when the can or bottle has been well agitated within the past several hours; the brew is a wheat beer; you are at a high altitude locale such as Denver; or the beer is coming out of an unusually gassy keg.

240   Two jogging scientists, wary of a magazine extolling the benefits of beer drinking for a jogger's health, said their research indicated that beer is little better than water for the healthy runner. Drs. Ralph Hall and Richard O'Kell, of Kansas City, took exception to an article in a national jogger's magazine written by heart specialist and runner, Dr. George Sheehan. Dr. Sheehan had suggested that beer was an excellent way to replace body fluids lost by perspiration because it contains only a few calories and a lot of potassium found in the body in the form of salt. But the pair of Kansas City doctors countered that it would require drinking 15 or more bottles of beer a day to provide the daily requirement.

241   An Aspen, Colorado newspaper, *The Times,* said drinking beer doesn't help the jogger's heart at all. "But it does improve their attitude."

242 Beer was included in a "full choice food plan" by Weight Watcher's International several years ago. Jane Hope, speaking for the weight-loss organization which was founded in 1962, said that because most dieters crave certain forbidden foods and beverages, they tend to fall off the diet wagon. The food plan allowed such "taboo" items—when in controlled portions—as beer, wine, champagne, peanut butter, popcorn, sweet potatoes, even raisins.

243 A diet book called "The I-Like-My-Beer-Diet" lists a daily menu program for breakfast, lunch and dinner and each day's menu includes beer. U.S. physician Martin R. Lipp wrote the book as a way for people to take off 10 or more pounds in 12 days. His high protein, low fat, low carbohydrate diet—based on a calorie intake of about 1,000 calories a day—allows two to three beers a day. He said beer has many advantages as a diet compound because it is filling and makes for a good late-night snack. He adds that beer is nutritious (rich in B-vitamins, including niacin) and it's relaxing, which helps people deal with the diet deprivation syndrome.

244 In 1983, the world's best-known bull was a full-grown, black Brahma bull that leaped through a wall in a TV beer commercial, sending splinters flying everywhere. The Schlitz Malt Liquor Bull (a hybrid of Brahma and Angus) was known as Jeckle, and the 1,800 lb. creature actually crashed through a set made of sugar glass, balsa wood and styrofoam bricks—nothing that would hurt the animal. One viewer, writing in *All About Beer* magazine, said the commercial was downright distracting. He wrote: "Every weekend millions of sports fans have the TV action broken by sixty seconds of bull-Schlitz, uh, Schlitz bull commercials."

245 In 1956, at the age of 81, Mickey O'Rourke, of Vancouver, returned home from the Victoria Cross Centenary Celebrations in London, England. The old warrior, who had been awarded the Commonwealth's premier military decoration for gallantry in recognition of the most exceptional bravery displayed in the presence of the enemy, said upon his return from the V.C. celebrations, "I've met the Queen. I've met the Princess Royal. I've met Sir Anthony Eden. But never once did I get a glass of Canadian beer."

246 In 1786, John Molson, of Montreal, said, "An honest brew makes its own friends."

247 When Colin Eastwood was manager of a Brewers Retail store in Oakville, Ontario, a representative of a local gun club came into the store and purchased 48 dozen cans of beer for a convention. Colin later described the sale as "a one shot deal".

248 The late Lawrence Porter was also a manager of a Brewers Retail store in Wiarton, Ontario. On one hot and sticky summer day, a customer entered his store, studied the vast display of brewers' products and asked the manager to name the best brand of beer. Without hesitation, Porter said, "My friend, the best brand of beer is the one that's good and cold and good and handy when you're good and thirsty."

249 In June, 1989, while visiting relatives in Bear River, Prince Edward Island, the author of *365 Beertime Stories* spotted the following poem on a plaque in the hallway

entrance of the home of his uncle Gerard McCloskey and his
wife, Celia:

"He grabbed me by my tapered neck
I couldn't yell or scream.
He took me to his dingy room
Where we could not be seen.
He stripped me of my flimsy wrap,
And gazed upon my form.
I was wet and cold and damp,
And he was nice and warm.
His feverish lips he pressed to mine,
I gave him every drop.
He drained me of my very self,
And I couldn't make him stop.
He made me what I am today,
That's why you find me here...
A broken bottle, tossed away,
That once was full of beer."

250 American writer James Lincoln Collier wrote an
essay called *My Love Affair With Beer* in which he said he has
drunk beer across the Old World, from Dublin to Moscow,
from Rome to Oslo. He declared that Canadian beer is "as
good as any."

251 A study of past and present beer advertising slogans
reveals the popularity of rhyming jingles in the promotion of
beer, such as: "It's Blended. It's Splendid" (Pabst Blue
Ribbon); "Taste Without Waist" (Black Label Beer, Brewing
Corp. of America); "The Toast of the Coast" (Aztec Brewing
Company).

252 One advertising slogan that has fallen victim to modern times is the little ditty dreamed up by the Potosi Brewing Company, in Missouri, whose celebrated boast was: "The beer that made the nineties gay."

253 A friend of Nancy McKerracher of Vancouver once discovered an empty bottle of beer in a newly-purchased case of Molson Old Style. The friend asked Nancy to compose a written complaint and send it to the brewery, along with the empty bottle with its cap still in place. The letter took the form of a poem in six verses. Here's the last one:

> "...so I have the job to write this complaint,
> And I do so with a smile,
> Not to be rude, unpleasant or snide.
> Just requesting another Old Style."

Molson's Marketing Manager at the time, S.C. Cara, rose to the occasion. Within a few days, Nancy and her friend received a cheque for the purchase price of a dozen pints and the following corporate reply:

> "We read your poem with mixed emotion,
> Those Old Style drinkers sure have devotion.
> It's nice to know you really care,
> But we're sad your bottle was filled with air.
>
> To make amends and even the score,
> Your bottle will be replaced by 12 more.
> To sell an empty bottle, there's no rhyme nor reason;
> In any event, have a happy Old Style season."

254 Doctors in Nottingham, England, believe that beer may have saved the life of a seriously-ill burn victim. The man had suffered extensive burns from a stove accident and was rapidly losing weight—in spite of intravenous feeding—when he mentioned to the staff of Nottingham City Hospital that he longed for his standard refreshment. "We would rather have given him milk, but he would only drink his favourite beer," said hospital administrator Christopher Wright. So, doctors allowed the man two pints a day and he began to improve immediately.

255 Steve Warden wrote an article in a California-based beer magazine that provided a historical overview of Canadian beer. "It just so happens that, when it comes to beer, Canada is a very appropriate place to live," wrote the author in *All About Beer* magazine. However, in one rather indiscreet paragraph, he talked about a Canadian tradition of teens entering bars with fake ID's. Warden said it's a tradition parents don't openly advocate but they "grin and bear it, and remember the times not so long ago when they trekked through the snow in their moccasins and parkas to sample their first taste of great Canadian brew."

256 Next time you're asked to raise a glass of beer and make a toast here's a popular 19th century toast that's a little more poetic than the old stand-by: "Cheers, here's mud in yer eye."

> "Let's drink the liquid of amber so bright;
> Let's drink the liquid with foam snowy white;
> Let's drink the liquid that brings all good cheer
> Oh, where is the drink like old-fashioned beer?"

257 If you'd prefer to be a little less eloquent in making your beer toasts, this one might be more appropriate:

> Who'd care to be a bee and sip
> Sweet honey from the flower's lip?
> When he might be a fly and steer
> Head first into a can of beer?"

258 Beer was not included in the U.S.-Canada free trade agreement that was signed by the two countries in 1988.

Before it was signed, Russell Cleary, board chairman and CEO of G. Heileman Brewing Co., criticized the Reagan administration for not placing restrictions against Canadian beer imports because of the barriers Canada implemented to block U.S. beer exports into Canada. But Canada argued successfully that large U.S. breweries have "idle capacity" to service the Canadian market and could sell beer with less expense than the Canadians. So, beer was not included in provisions for improved treatment of U.S. liquor exports to Canada.

259 Le Chaudiere pub in Hull, Quebec, can serve 3,500 beer drinkers at one sitting.

260 Leonard Louis Levinson penned this thoughtful proverb:

> "He that buys land buys many stones,
> He that buys flesh buys many bones.
> He that buys eggs buys many shells,
> But he that buys good ale buys nothing else."

261 Six million empty beer bottles were once shipped from Halifax, Nova Scotia, to West Africa. The freighter's captain explained that bottles were in big demand in Nigeria where bottled beer at the time was considered "something of a status symbol."

262 Moosehead beer is a beer from Eastern Canada. In Ontario, several years ago, a brewery transport truck hit a moose on Highway 11, near the northern community of Cochrane. No, the truck was not carrying Moosehead beer.

263 During World War II, Canadian Prime Minister Mackenzie King issued a request that Canadians drink less. Beer baron and financier E.P. Taylor, who formed the Brewing Corp. of Canada Ltd. (later Canadian Breweries), issued this press statement in 1941, as a response: "A plentiful supply of it can make an important contribution to the well-being of the nation."

264 On a cold night in the northern Ontario community of Spanish, north of Manitoulin Island, police received a call from a man who said he'd just broken into the local beer store, stolen some beer, and would they please come and pick him up. Police found the man walking down the road drinking beer. "What the hell kept you?" he asked the police. "Don't you realize how cold it is out here?" They whisked him off to a warm jail cell.

265 The city of Brussels takes itself seriously and what the city is most serious about is its beer. An important staple of Belgian cuisine, as many as 700 brands of beer are available in the cafes throughout the city. The Belgians are not only serious about producing beer, they rank with the Czechs and Germans as the most dedicated drinkers of their brews, according to writer Greg Byers. In an article written from Brussels, Byers also noted that protocol governs the shape of the glass from which one drinks and the kind of meal appropriate for certain beer.

266 If you're looking for a book for the man or woman who has everything, here's one you might consider, *The Complete Book of Beer Drinking Games*. Written by three Yale University graduates, the book provides rules for 50 beer drinking games, including "The Beer Hunter" and "Zoom, Schwartz and Perfigliano." Written in a humourous style, it takes care to caution players not to drink and drive if they play any of the games listed.

267 Many pubs in working class areas have what is called a Happy Hour. However, if the pub is located in a "high stress" downtown area, some pub owners prefer to call it the "attitude adjustment hour" and if the pub is situated in a ritzy part of town, don't be surprised to hear it referred to as the establishment's "Social Adjustment Hour."

268 Former National Hockey League great, Gordie Howe, was known for his elbow work in the corners, his longevity in the sport, and his cunning play on the ice. But the *Montreal Gazette* reported that only a privileged few ever saw him, on the overnight train from Montreal to Detroit, open an entire case of 24 with his teeth when it was discovered no one had thought to bring a bottle opener.

269 Beer and wine expert Richard Nagel said beer is taking on a new sophistication. The New York wine cellar master began working for the prestigious Vista International Hotel in the 1960's, helping restaurants establish their beer and wine operations. Recently, he said beer isn't for picnics anymore. "The right beer — for example, a quality super premium such as Lowenbrau — is a good complement for so many foods, including trendy, spicy foods," he said. "It's time for restaurateurs to consider beer, like wine, as a perfect match for fine restaurant meals."

270 Two Canadian beer companies were among the country's top 10 spenders on advertising, in 1987. John Labatt Limited was in 5th spot, having spent $36 million to advertise its diverse products and The Molson Companies was 9th, spending $28.8 million to tell people about its many products.

271 The longest recorded one-man chain of can tops is one of 11.2 miles, collected since July 4, 1969, by Arthur J. Jordan Sr., of Yorkstown, Virginia. It took Mr. Jordan 10 years to collect 710,000 can tops.

272 Oscar Wilde wasn't known as a beer drinker but that didn't stop a California brewery from naming a beer after the 19th century homosexual English author. The beer, brewed specifically for homosexuals, was test-marketed in San Diego in 1984. Wilde's Brewing Co. chairman, Lee Nichol, said 35% of the profits from sales would be turned over to the homosexual community. "Wilde might have only drunk a beer on a warm day in Italy," said Nichols, "but he was gay and he did have a sense of style."

273 Music legend Chuck Berry made his first appearance on a can of beer in 1984, pictured in the stance familiar to rock-and-roll fans since the 1950's. Berry was invited to St. Louis to receive the first case of Rock & Roll beer when the new can was introduced. "The whole point is to honour him,"

said rock music historian, tavern owner and Rock & Roll
Beer founder, Joe Edwards.

274 Some anti-drinking messages are so hard-hitting they
lose their effectiveness and purpose, so it's nice to see a
gentle ad once in awhile that encourages moderation in
alcohol consumption. The gentlest one around is the slogan
of Phoenix Imports, Ltd. of Ellicott City, Md. The U.S.
importers of several beers, including Thomas Hardy's Ale
and Royal Oak Pale Ale, promoted a slogan in 1989 that was
printed on what looked like a triangular-shaped road sign.
The message? "Drink gently."

275 The Great Canadian Beer Book tells the story of a
33-inch fish, caught in Lake St. Clair, that seemed a tad too
heavy for its size. When they popped the fish's top, startled
fishermen found a full bottle of ale inside the creature.

276 Budweiser appeared to be capturing the imagination
and taste of the international beer market in the mid-80's,
according to *Business Week Magazine.* An article introduced
Graham Nott, 25, and his rugby-playing mates in the southern
English village of Turnbridge Wells who liked to relax after
their Sunday matches at the 16th century Hole-in-the-Wall
pub. Shunning dozens of traditional dark and heavy beers
that line the wood-panelled bar, Nutt and his buddies were
turning more and more to Budweiser. "It's a nice drop of
beer, easy to drink," said Nott. The magazine article noted
also that a continent away, in Tokyo's Jack and Betty pub,
19-year-old Yuko Takahashi was also singing the praises of
Budweiser. "It gives you a feeling of a beer for the young," she
said.

277 "The best thing for you," the doctor said to his ailing patient, "is to give up drinking beer, quit smoking, stop womanizing and get to bed early every night." The man answered, "I don't deserve the best, doc. What's second best?"

278 A man came home very late one night with the odour of beer on his breath. He was confronted by his angry wife. "I want an explanation and I want the truth," she demanded. Her husband replied, "Make up your mind. You can't have both."

279 Banning pitchers of beer from bars might help reduce drinking and driving, said a psychology professor at Virginia Polytechnic Institute and State University in Blacksburg. "People don't want as much beer as they get in that pitcher," said professor Scott Geller. But they figure it's cheaper and feel compelled to "clean the plate." He found that on average, bar patrons drank 35 ounces of beer per person when it came in a pitcher, but only 15 ounces from a bottle and 12 ounces from a glass.

280 When the Amstel Brewery in Hamilton, Ontario, introduced a new brand of beer called Grizzly, the normally staid *Globe and Mail* (Canada's "national" newspaper) ran the following item: "If you go down in the woods today, you may be in for a big surprise--a new beer called Grizzly. After one bottle, they say, you feel like hugging someone; after two, you start climbing trees."

281 The 1984 *Good Beer Guide* told British beer drinkers they were getting a weaker pint and paying more for it. Neil

Hanson, editor of the guide that ranks pubs throughout Britain, said the beer industry was "riddled with overcharging" both by brewers and pub owners, and that the venerable British pub had become a dirty and indifferent place. Hanson's attack on pubs included this opinion: "Too many pubs are the equivalent of bad motorway service stations, offering vinegary beer, indifferent service and dirty surroundings."

282 The green beer bottle has to go, declared a group dedicated to better beer drinking. The Campaign for Authentic Beer said in 1983 that an Australian study described — for the first time — the harm done by artificial light in grocery stores and display cases on beer bottled in anything other than brown glass. The study showed that a brown glass blocks fluorescent light that can give beer a "skunky" flavour. "People think a green bottle means a higher quality beer, but it's just the opposite," said Larry Popelka, who was president of the 500-member group. He added that the green bottle craze is un-American.

283 A group of psychologists in Britain suggested that youngsters in prison should get 20 pints of beer a day — for free. The doctors wanted to set up bars in prisons, believing that binges would help young offenders learn to control excessive drinking. "First you need to get them on a bender," said psychologist Dr. Clive Hollin, in a 1983 interview. "Once you find out how much they really drink, you can teach them to control themselves."

284 Newspaper columnist McKenzie Porter said every good pub must have an instantly recognizable publican, otherwise known as the landlord or the "mine host." Porter said such hosts "whose standards of service and comportment impart to the precincts a unique aspect, are artists in the creation of convivial atmosphere." He told of one London landlord who used to charge newcomers what he called "face money." This involved demanding a supplement to the bill from all persons whose face did not arouse his instant admiration. Porter admitted, "My own face cost me a pound each time, until I proved I could spread a smile."

285 On the morning after the death of Edward VII, the editor of the *Yorkshire Post* wrote that "if His Majesty had not been king, he would have made a perfect publican."

286 When Fred Uzzell turned 100, he said the secret to a long life is "shooting the bull" and "beer — one every night before bed." At his centennial birthday party on July, 13, 1983 at Toronto's Sunnybrook Medical Centre, Uzzell said, "I still love to dance the can-can and I've got my regular bottle of beer every night." His daughter, Mabel, said they had to move her father to another wing of the hospital because in the area where he was, they went to bed too early for him.

287 The longest permanent bar in the world is the 340-ft.long bar in Lulu's Roadhouse, Kitchener, Ontario, which opened April 3, 1984. The Working Men's Club bar at Mildura, Victoria, Australia, has a counter 298 feet long and serves beer from 27 pumps.

288 The largest beer-selling establishment in the world is the Mathaser, Bayerstrasse 5, in Munich, West Germany, which seats 5,500 and the daily sale reaches 100,000 pints. Consumption at the Dube beer halls in the Bantu township of Soweto, Johannesburg, South Africa, is an average of 57,280 pints (7,160 gallons) of beer on some Saturdays.

289 Ladies-in-waiting at the court of King Henry VIII were allowed a gallon of beer a day—for breakfast.

290 The first beer can was test-marketed by Krueger Bee of Richmond, Va., in 1935.

291 Canada's natives are said to have made beer from spruce trees. The concoction was said to possess certain medicinal properties and, it is claimed, saved the lives of explorer Jacques Cartier's crew when they staggered ashore with scurvy in 1597.

292 A reader of the *Winnipeg Free Press* asked why so many Canadian beer bottles are made from brown glass. Before giving a straight answer, the reply in the June 3, 1983 question-and-answer column began this way: "If beer bottles weren't brown, we couldn't refer to them as little brown soldiers. As well, the colour helps serious imbibers tell the difference between a beer (which is good to drink) and a vase of flowers (which is not so good to drink)."

293 The Paris publication, *Le Monde,* carried a full-page advertisement for beer entirely in Latin in its April 21, 1983 edition. Under the heading *De abbatia quadam in Belgica sita cervisia-rumque generibus ab ea nominatis* (this is about a certain abbey in Belgium and the types of beers named after it), the advertisement extolled the delights of the beer and challenged Latin scholars to look for clues in coming days to win prizes.

294 In a subway, a crowd is called congestion; in a bar, it's called atmosphere.

295 "Revellers coiffed their beverage of choice from cans, wine skins, bottles or plastic cups." Coiffed? This little gem appeared in *The Toronto Star* on January 1, 1989, in a story about New Year's Eve celebrations at the City Hall Square. It was caught and corrected to "quaffed" but not before some editions went out to *Star* readers. A few days later, H.M. Kershaw wrote to ask, "Do we put this down to the morning after?" He sketched a coiffured beer mug to go along with his critique.

296 West Germans may think of beer as "liquid bread" but there's one chimpanzee teetotaler who visited the Bavarian capital with a circus, and angrily refused a free drink. The chimp not only turned down the beer but attacked the man who offered it to him. Police said the primate bit off one of the man's fingers, broke his arm and scratched his face. The man, who described himself as a friend of apes, climbed over a barrier at the circus in a Munich suburb, approached the chimpanzee's cage, reached through the bars and offered the chimp a full bottle of beer. The chimp grabbed the man's extended arm instead of the bottle.

297 Curling is one of Canada's favorite national winter sports. One of the world's best curlers is Glenn Howard who won the Men's World Championship of Curling in 1987, along with his three team-mates. On April 5th, the team beat a German foursome in the finals in Vancouver, B.C., which was watched by millions of television viewers around the globe. Less than 48-hours after sweeping the world title, Glenn was back at his job as a beer store manager in Barrie, Ontario.

298 Darrell George was also a beer store manager for the same Ontario company, Brewers Retail, when he won a title of a different kind. After a Toronto photographer "discovered" Darrell walking along a Jamaican beach, he was asked if he would consider posing as one of the *Toronto Sun* newspaper's daily Sunshine Boys. Darrell agreed, and a photo of the 24-year-old manager of the Havelock beer store appeared on page three of the daily newspaper. In subsequent judging by the paper's readers, Darrell was named the paper's Sunshine Boy-of-the-Month for January and, ultimately, Sunshine Boy-of-the-Year for 1986. He received $1,000 for the honour. Debbie Brown, who also worked for Brewers Retail until May, 1989 at their Toronto Head Office, was featured as the paper's Sunshine Girl-of-the-Day on December 31, 1985. A Human Resources Secretary at the time, she was voted the paper's Sunshine Girl-of-the-Month and became the first runner-up for Sunshine Girl-of-the-Year.

299 The Brewers Retail corporate magazine, *Kegs & Cases,* once asked the children of its employees what they thought their parents did at work. Five-year-old Heather Mayor said her dad "sells beer, cleans up, makes money, unloads beer, piles beer, locks the doors at night, and opens the store." When asked who buys beer, she replied, "People. And they are old." Another youngster, Jay Tipping, 8, said, "My dad works at the Brewers Retail. I think he carries beer for the women. He gives people money for their empty bottles. At lunchtime he sometimes sleeps on the beer cases because he works so hard. I would like to help my dad when I am old enough."

300 When Australia lost the world drinking record to Germany in 1978 (the Aussie's annual beer consumption was 36 gallons per capita to the German's 38 gallons), a *Toronto Sun* newspaper article on September 21, 1979, lent its support to "Aussiland's" beer drinkers. It noted: "Swan's bronze cans are the nicest in the world. Crush 'em with two fingers and impress the bazoobies out of girls."

301 Kathleen Crowley, of Burlington, Ontario, once travelled the world visiting breweries and sampling their products. Then she wrote a book titled, *All The Free Beer You Can Drink*. Essentially it's a guide book to breweries around the world. "The toughest part of writing the book was to stay sober and to stay skinny," said the author who was in her 20's when she tackled the assignment. When the slim, tawny-haired beauty approached her publisher with the idea for the book, they were taken aback. "They seemed to think I should be an Australian named Bruce," she recalled.

302 If you're driving down the road and see a car with licence plates BREW 4 U, you'll know you're following Steve Rohr. Steve was a beer store manager in Mississauga, Ontario, when he paid $100 for the personalized plates. "A lot of people wave to me on the road," he said.

303 *The Dictionary of Canadian Quotations and Phrases* quotes Bob Edwards, who wrote in the *Calgary Eye Opener* on July 8, 1916, during the height of World War I: "Sold honestly and in an open and aboveboard manner, temperance beer will just fill the bill nicely and keep the boys satisfied and contented."

304 Dry beer first made its splash in Japan. Dry beer's main feature in the Land of the Rising Sun is that it is stronger than the average Japanese brew and doesn't leave a lingering aftertaste. Its alcohol content is 5% as against the usual 4.5%. This makes it slightly less sweet than regular beer. In the summer of 1988, demand for the wonder brew outstripped production to such an extent that Asahi Breweries forbade its employees to buy it and some Tokyo liquor stores had to ration their supplies.

305   The Upper Canada Brewing Company became the first North American brewer in 471 years to have its product imported into that bastion of great beers - Germany. The relatively new Toronto brewery claimed the distinction when it shipped 1,050 cases of its all-natural ingredient lager, ale, and True Light brands to Germany, Holland, Belgium and Luxembourg in 1987. Upper Canada Brewery was accepted for importation into West Germany when it was judged as meeting the rigid standards set down in the Bavarian Purity Law of 1516.

306   Incredibly, through word-of-mouth advertising, the Mexican beer brand Corona Export became the second-largest selling import beer in the United States in

1987. But in 1988, sales fizzled when a false — but persistent — rumour was spread that the beer was contaminated with urine. Another problem was that Corona was perceived as the yuppie beer despite research that showed the beverage enjoyed a very broad user base, according to its importer Barton Brands. A Barton spokesman said in August, 1988, "This year, there is a very real anti-yuppie feeling throughout the country and, because of the handle hung on the brand (by the media), we are suffering a bit of a backlash."

307 Venezuela's best-selling beer, Polar beer, made inroads in the United States in 1988 with a sexy — some say sexist — marketing campaign focusing on the beer's long-necked bottle and fired-on white label. In its first television commercial, a woman is shown running her fingers down the neck of a Polar bottle and saying, "What a bottle." That stirred up critics such as Adweek, which in its annual "Badvertising" report, cited it as an example of bad taste.

308 When Andrew Plum operated Plums Pub and Dart Emporium on Toronto's Mount Pleasant Blvd., he claimed that his store carried one of the largest collections of pub paraphernalia in the world. In the summer of 1986, at Plum's, you could buy a 1902 unopened bottle of beer (King's Ale) for $250; a Carling Black Label beer tray for $2.50; a pair of Guinness cuff links for $45; or an assortment of draft beer handles priced at $18 — to name a few items. Part of their business came from renting pub paraphernalia for TV commercials and movies. A Montreal film company was making a movie in Yugoslavia and needed a 1930's type of British bar. They bought it at Plums.

309 Howard Hillman, who travelled to 100 countries in his search for the perfect beer, said he believes the world's most popular alcoholic beverage is worthy of connoisseurship. So, he wrote a book called *The Gourmet Guide To Beer* and dedicated it to "lovers of quality beer". The author said he didn't write it for beer snobs nor for the undiscriminating six-pack guzzlers. Rather, he wrote the handbook for "the individual who shares my unwavering conviction that quality beer deserves our consuming passion in the full figurative sense." Maintaining that beer is just as complex, varied and exciting as wine, he admonishes the public for having learned the rudiments of wine appreciation, while remaining unversed in the finer points of beer.

310 There are several thousand different beers in the world and Michael Jackson has tasted a good number of them. The Yorkshire, England, author of several books on beer, including the World Guide To Beer, believes he's visited more breweries than anyone else in the world. "There's not much doubt I've tasted more beer than any other man alive," said Jackson, who estimated in a 1988 interview with Terry Gilbert of the Calgary Herald, that the number is well into the thousands. An unapologetic beer snob, he named Corona, from Mexico, as the worst beer he has tasted. He added he has difficulty keeping the number of his favourite beers to 20. He named Portland and Seattle as good spots for a beer-tasting trip, calling them "the two most beer conscious cities in the U.S."

311 James D. Robertson and a panel of taste testers sampled more than 1,350 brews in a quest to discover the best in the world. After the monumental taste-test (it goes without saying the man is in love with his job!), a short list of 200 brews qualified for a final taste-off. The results of Robertson's beer honour roll appeared in his book, The Connoisseur's Guide To Beer published in 1984. He said the most important fact he learned about beer after over a thousand brands, is that it is a fragile commodity, just like wine. But he said beer drinking can be a rewarding experience if handled with care and thought. And he added, "Beer should be enjoyed without stigma. In most of the world it is regarded as a food and it certainly has a long record of success as a means of promoting temperance."

312 King Hammurabi, of Babylon, worried that his subjects might raise the roof if beer got any costlier, imposed a price ceiling.

313 On page 94 of Big Bob's Beautiful Beer Book, there is a full-page cartoon of a sleepy-eyed individual saying, "Every morning I get up and make coffee in my pajamas. Some day I'll try a coffee pot." Interspersed between cartoons and recipes, the whimsical book also provides valuable "references" for beer lovers. Author Robert Dawson describes the pouring of beer as a pleasure unto itself, "Just watching the golden liquid bubble up and turn into a frothing head arouses our senses. A beer without a head is like a pencil without a point."

314 One of Quebec's most respected historical figures, M. Jean Talon, said in 1668 that beer was vital to New France "to provide a wholesome alternative to strong distilled spirits."

315 The Brewers Association of Canada once ran an ad that gave a historical perspective on our "humble brew's distinguished and illustrious past." A heading over the print ad read: "Canadians didn't invent beer — they just perfected it." Among a series of vignettes and beer anecdotes, was this item: "Even Canadian humourist Stephen Leacock took time to contemplate some of life's more serious concerns. Certainly, it was one of those moments that moved him to record this sentiment'...that a cup of ale beneath a tree is better than a civic banquet.'"

316 Some beer experts say there are 5,000 different beers in the world. Others have said there are between 15,000 and 20,000. Whatever the number, there's probably a beer for every letter of the alphabet, from Norway's Aas-bok beer to Zwyiec, a honey golden hoppy drink brewed in Poland.

317 Does your bartender dip the tip of the spigot into the draft beer when refilling your glass? If so, ask him to stop. Many beer experts believe this to be unhygienic because germs from someone else's dirty glass could be transferred to the spigot and eventually to your glass.

318 In many countries — even in regions and pubs within certain areas — beer glasses differ appreciably from one another. In Germany, for example, most of the large brewers commission designers to custom-design beer vessels for their brews. While some artists utilize glass in their creations, others prefer earthenware steins. In Munich's Hofbrauhaus, for example, the tapmen use earthenware steins exclusively. According to beer expert H. Berberoglu, a professor of hospitality and tourism at Ryerson Polytechnical Institute in Toronto, earthenware steins are popular in Bavaria but glassware is preferred in Berlin. Some of the popular shaped glasses in that city include pilsen-style, balloon-shaped, and flute-shaped glasses, as well as bowl style.

319 "Beer money" was payment of a penny a day to British soldiers in lieu of issue of beer or spirits, established in 1800 and abolished in 1873. This and other explanations of beer syntax appears in the *Dictionary of Drink and Drinking* by Oscar A. Mendelsohn. He says "ship's beer" was the common term used well into the 19th century for the strong beer supplied to ships. "Beerage" is the rather snobbish and derogatory allusion to the fact that many English brewers have been raised to the peerage. "Beer and skittles" is synonymous for good living—drink and play.

320 Belinda Metz, of Edmonton, Alberta, was a Cinderella queen. The young lady sang and danced her way into the hearts of judges at a Miss Oktoberfest contest held in Kitchener-Waterloo, Ontario. The five-foot, four-inch, 123-pound beauty was crowned queen of the Twin Cities beerfest and for nine days and nights she toured most of the festive beer halls without once touching a drop of beer to her lips. Belinda was 17-years-old and under the drinking age.

321 In 1972, a female customer at The Brickskeller, in Washington, D.C., bet owner Maurice Coja he couldn't get her a Coors beer. Coors is made in Denver, and she figured distance was on her side. The lady won the bet. Coja admitted he couldn't get it for her right away but promised he'd have it the following week. He bought a refrigeration truck and sent out a driver with it to bring back a case of Coors. "And bring back any other cases you find on the way," Coja ordered. A dozen years later, the Brickskeller, at 1523 22nd Street, was carrying 510 different brands of beer.

322 Robert Seysmith wrote in a hotel and restaurant magazine: "Beer, since it is largely taken for granted, has perhaps been under-exploited in terms of being a taste-pleasing as well as a thirst-quenching beverage."

323 Beer drinkers at Toronto's Rotterdam Brewpub have a choice of 27 varieties of draft beer and can choose from a selection of 348 bottled beers, most of them imported. One Swiss beer wields a demonic jolt—an alcohol content of 12%.

324 When John Mitchell decided to open a brewpub in British Columbia in the early 1980's, he was reminded by the province's Liquor Board that rules stated a brewpub's beer must be draft, it must not be bottled. That law was fine with Mitchell since his beer would be devoid of chemicals that prolong shelf life so it needed to be drunk right away. Richer and maltier, made from 100% barley mash and with no adjuncts like rice and corn to keep the starch up and production costs down, it wouldn't travel well, anyway. "It's a neurotic beer," said Mitchell. "It's also got more calories, more body; we're the cakes of the industry; everything else is Wonderbread."

325 In one of his books on beer, Ryerson tourism and hospitality professor H. Berberoglu, said testing beer is an "organoleptic" exercise. To assist his "students of beer" with their homework, the author provided dozens of descriptive terms, from A to Z, that are used to describe beer, from "ambrosial" (outstanding; a pleasant aftertaste) to "zesty" (lively and piquant; invigorating.)

326 Holding a beer taste-off can be a tough job, said Will Anderson, author of From Beer To Eternity. "And, done with care and patience, can take several hours." He said at least eight to ten brews should be used, making sure there are a range of types. Each beer should be rated for appearance, aroma, taste and aftertaste. Devise a rating scale of 0-4 and cleanse the palate with a cracker and a little cheese. When all of the beer has been sampled and rated for each characteristic, add up everyone's total scores. Eliminate the lowest ranking four or five, and repeat the taste test using only the top four or five beers left. To build drama, said Anderson, (as well as to provide a fine excuse to enjoy more beer) keep on going until you've narrowed the brews down to the best three, the best two and finally, the best one. "Kiss it, crown it, tie a ribbon around it...do something to declare it the winner!"

327 Two thieves who put booze ahead of money broke into a bank by mistake but corrected their error by raiding the adjoining beer and liquor stores. "I think they went into the bank by mistake, thinking it was the beer store," said acting Sgt. Dennis Judd of the Ingersoll, Ontario, police department. The thieves stole a few cases of liquor and four cases of beer from the liquor and beer outlets. It was believed they used a crowbar to pry open air vents on the roofs of the stores. Police said the thieves were in a storeroom in the bank when they realized their mistake.

328 Molson Golden and Molson Export were ranked highly in a 1988 taste test of more than 40 brands of imported beer, by *L.A. Style* magazine for a feature article called *A Jury Of Your Beers*. The writer called the two Canadian beer "a favorite of our panel, with an attractive nose and a tasty, pert butterscotch flavor." Molson Golden received an "outstanding" rating, only one of two beer to earn that top rating. Other top notch brews were New Zealand's Steinlager and Japan's Kirin Beer.

329 Six Munich-based breweries traditionally have the right to take part in the city's famous 16-day beerfest that attracts seven million visitors each year. And every year, breweries from outside the town try to get in. But even royal brewers are kept at bay. Bavarian Prince Luitpold, whose ancestors founded the Oktoberfest, has been refused permission to set up a hut because his brewery, Kaltenberg, is outside Munich. Luitpold's ancestor, Ludwig I of Bavaria, launched the Oktoberfest to celebrate his marriage to Princess Therese von Sachsen-Hildburghausen in October, 1810. The first festival took place in a field in Munich and the beer tents have been erected there ever since.

330 Les Jessop, former brewing chief of Canadian Breweries, once compared Canadians' preference in their taste for beer to the European and American taste, with these words: "We enjoy something a little milder. Less bitter. You can taste the hops more in European beer. The Canadian hop character is delicate. However, there is more fullness in our beer than in American beer — the feeling of having a real mouthful."

331 A large Soviet vessel lifted anchor in Montreal, June 3, 1987, and headed for Leningrad with a new Canadian export product in its hold--beer. Seven containers of Molson Canadian beer were loaded on the Starostenko. Jacques Allard, president of Molson Brewery Quebec Ltd., noted that the 201,600 cans of beer were a trial shipment. The beer went on sale the next month in Moscow foreign currency stores. At a ceremony on deck, prior to lifting anchor for the voyage, beer and vodka was used to toast the shipment. The ship's captain, Genady Larionov, was asked jokingly if all the beer would arrive at its destination. He gestured with his bottle and smiled, "Don't worry about that. All will be delivered in good condition."

332 David Kuntz emigrated to Canada from Germany well over a century ago and settled in Waterloo, Ontario. Typical of the people who came from Germany at that time, Kuntz was a craftsman, a brewer and a brickmaker. The founder of the Carling O'Keefe Brewery, he made all of the bricks used for his first brewery and they remain in good condition today. Kuntz brewed beer during the day, loaded his wagon with kegs of the amber beverage brewed earlier and delivered it around the countryside in an ox-drawn wagon. Selling beer was a cash business at that time and he carried large sums of money. As a precaution against hold-ups, it is believed that he used to hide the money in an empty beer keg on the wagon.

333 North Americans enjoy their beer cold, clear and sparkly. The Genesee Brewing Company knew that fact only too well when it discovered several winters ago that it had nearly 600,000 gallons of "cloudy" beer and ale. The Rochester brewery didn't want the stuff so it was sent back to the canner, an American Can plant in suburban Fairport. A

Genesee spokesman explained how the problem occurred: "A compound that was used to seal the tops and bottoms of the beer cans reacted with the beer, causing the protein in the cans to come together in small strings. The beer was safe to drink, you couldn't taste anything different and it was even hard to notice in a glass. It just didn't meet our quality standards." The beer and ale, which had a retail value of $1.5 million, eventually ended up in the Monroe County sewer system. After meeting with county officials, American Can started dumping the suds into sewers at a rate of 5,000 gallons a day. In four months it was all gone and even though American Can reportedly lost $1 million, they, too, realized there was no use crying over spilled beer.

334 Glen Allen was able to add another room to his house, a number of years ago, and he didn't even have to lift a hammer. All he did was clear the room of 408 cases of empty beer bottles and — presto — an empty workroom. Allen and four of his friends loaded the beer cases onto pick-up trucks and took them to a beer store in Kitchener, Ontario. The refund on the returnable bottles amounted to nearly $500. Allen had been collecting the beer bottles for three years. At first, when he had 20 cases, he was going to turn them in for a refund but thought he'd "keep going." He might have kept on accumulating the cases but he needed the space for a "special project."

335 A judge in Brisbane, Australia, once suggested that warnings against rape be put on beer cans, hamburger shops and driver's licences. Sentencing two youths to seven years in jail for raping an 11-year-old girl, Judge Skerman said there was evidence linking driving and the availability of cars, with multiple rape cases by young men. He suggested that the warnings read: "The penalty for rape is high."

336 Water was not the only natural ingredient that was used to brew beer when Anheuser-Busch turned to the sun in Jacksonville, Florida, one year, for the heat needed to pasteurize beer. The solar pasteurization unit was the first such use of solar energy by the beer industry and one of the first industrial applications of the sun's heat in the U.S. At a dedication ceremony, then-chairman and president August A. Busch III, said the project would give Anheuser-Busch the information it needed to plan energy systems for future plants. Heat from the sun, collected by rooftop solar cells, was used to produce a temperature of more than 140 degrees F. in water sprayed on bottles of beer as they moved through the pasteurizer. The system was designed to replace conventional heating systems for one of seven pasteurizing units at the Jacksonville brewery.

337 Every now and then someone suggests that the Canadian brewing industry be forced to list all beer ingredients on beer labels. Newspaper reporter Evan Evans-Atkinson once said every time it is mentioned, "the brewing industry whips itself into a froth."

338 Forty-three thousand drinkers signed a petition in January, 1977, calling for the sale of hard liquor in British Columbia beer parlours. Provincial regulations at the time were worded to permit the sale of liquor in beer parlours but the government minister in charge of liquor sales, Rafe Mair, was not swayed by the magnitude of the petition. He said sales would continue to be forbidden as a matter of government policy.

339 In order to settle all the bar room arguments about which beer was the best in America in 1978, *Newsweek Magazine* assembled a "panel of experts" consisting solely of its Chicago Bureau Chief Frank Maier. After many hours of thoroughly unscientific research and a suitable rest period thereafter, Maier drew up his ratings. Following, minus his detailed explanations, are some of the winners and losers in Mr. Maier's personal Beer Olympics in the fall of '78:

BEST OF THE BIGGIES:	Budweiser
MOST OVER-RATED:	Coors
MOST UNDER-RATED:	Heileman's Old Style
COMEBACK OF THE YEAR:	Schlitz
BLANDEST:	Miller High Life
MOST DISAPPOINTING:	Lowenbrau
BEST OF THE LIGHTS:	Miller's Light and Pabst Extra Light
THE GUZZLER'S CHOICE:	Pabst Blue Ribbon, Schaefer, or Iron City
BEST FOR THE BOSS:	Heineken or St. Pauli Girl (from Germany)
BEST FOR SIPPING:	Heileman's Special Export
MOST 'IN' ON CAMPUS:	Stroh's
BEST OF THE LOCAL BRANDS:	Leinenkugel's
SAFEST CHOICE:	Olympia
MOST INTERESTING IMPORT:	Pilsner Urquell (a Czech beer)
BEST FIRE EXTINGUISHER:	Dos Equis, from Mexico (for spicy foods)
WETTEST:	Schoen's Old Lager
THE WORST:	Billy Beer

340 Herb Caen once reported in his column in the San Francisco Chronicle on the best and worst booze in China, saying that beer is the most palatable beverage in China, not tea, as most people might think. He claimed the best, by far, is Tsing-tao (pronounced "tchung-tchoe"). Caen said the worst drink by far is Mao-tai, China's famous 120-proof revenge on the free world. He warned it is to be avoided at any cost "even when it's free."

341 When one of the largest supply vessels ever built under the U.S. flag was christened in Houma, Louisiana, a bottle of Budweiser beer was broken against the hull, instead of the traditional bottle of champagne.

342 In 1937, a bill was passed in Quebec stating women would be "tolerated" in taverns. The bill was quickly squelched, however, due to an overwhelming number of complaints.

343 A Canadian is a person who lives in Canada, and not a 12-ounce bottle of beer, a Federal Court of Appeal ruled in 1988. The court refused to let Molson Companies Ltd. register the word "Canadian" as a trademark for one of its most popular brands of beer, Molson Canadian. The court had earlier ruled that the company could not register its Golden brand, since golden is a colour and an adjective which could describe any beer.

344 It took nine months to research the *Great Canadian Beer Book*, in 1975, and when it was published a luncheon was held at one of the country's busiest taverns, The Brunswick House in Toronto. The media, including a photographer from *Time Magazine* and a CBC television crew, turned out in full force to film and interview the book's authors, Gerald Donaldson and Gerald Lampert. The photographers were hampered from doing their job, however, by a Liquor Control Board of Ontario rule that prohibited the taking of pictures inside a place that serves liquor.

345 *The Toronto Star* published an item on September 14, 1980, about famed Toronto publicist for entertainers, Gino Empry. *The Star* said Empry sent singer Paul Williams to Dr. Simon McGrath "who delighted Williams by telling him to drink beer to loosen his vocal chords."

346 Beer seems to bring out the best (or worst) in newspaper headline writers. "Try to grin and beer it" and "Canadian firms at lagerheads in fight for U.S. beer market" are two such samples. On one day, March 18, 1988, two rival Toronto newspapers ran these heady headlines: "Ninety-nine battles of beer" (*Toronto Globe and Mail*) "Brewery stays on tap of things" (*Toronto Sun*).

347 Signs have been used to advertise businesses for thousands of years, according to John Cook, one of England's foremost authorities on signs, who calls them "the repository of our social history." In past centuries it was important to identify drinking establishments, for example, although few of the masses could read or write. The obvious and simplest way to proclaim a type of business was to have some form of pictorial sign attached to the premises. In 1392, Richard II compelled publicans, by law, to exhibit a sign. The law stated:

"Whosoever shall brew ale in the town with intention of selling it must hang out a sign, otherwise he shall forfeit his ale."

348 In the 14th century in England, an Ale-garland had to be hung outside an inn whenever a new brew was to be offered for sale. The purpose of the garland was to draw the attention of the official Ale-taster, or Ale-conner, to the fact that a new brew was ready for examination. These civic officials had the authority to examine each fresh brew and "retailer's measure" to ensure that it was sold at proper prices. If the Ale-conner deemed the brew to be adulterated or below standard, the vendor would be taken before the magistrate. Punishment ranged from a fine to a dunking in the river. Sometimes the punishment was made to fit the crime and an injunction was obtained to force the "culprit" to drink as much of the bad ale as he could hold. The remainder of the brew was then poured over him.

349 This popular 19th century toast is often adapted to the use of a particular brand of beer, such as the following from a St. Louis brewery:

> "Let's drink the liquid of amber so bright;
> Let's drink the liquid with foam snowy white;
> Let's drink the liquid that brings all good cheer;
> Oh, where is the drink like Lemp's Lager Beer?"

350 On Super Bowl Sunday, 1987, a female bull terrier with the unmarketable name of Honey Tree Evil Eye made her national television debut under the alias Spuds MacKenzie. According to Michael Roarty, a veteran executive of Anheuser-Busch, no one knows or pretends to know what made this particular mutt such a great beer "salesperson." Roarty explained to *Sports Illustrated Magazine,* in August, 1988, how the phenomenon got started: "Some guy in our Chicago agency drew a rough sketch of a dog, called the Party Animal, for a Bud Light poster. That meant we had to find a real dog that looked like his drawing. That meant Spuds. Orders for the poster of this strange-looking dog were monumental. We still can't explain it. It's like everything else in advertising. You just hope you get it right, but you never know for sure." Since Spuds first went on the air during the '87 Super Bowl, she has appeared in a dozen different commercials. Bud Light's sales rose 21% in 1987, by volume the biggest jump of any brand in the business.

351 The Idler Pub on Toronto's Davenport Road is known as a literary pub "where people who write, meet." Patrons can be seen sketching, writing, or reading one of the many publications that are offered in the pub's "newsstand" including *Pravda,* the *International Herald Tribune, Village Voice, Harpers, Literary Review, New Yorker Magazine* and daily copies of the *New York Times.* On the 2nd floor of the pub, a serious literary magazine, *The Idler,* is published six times a year. When David Warren was editor and publisher of the 9,000-circulation magazine he'd sometimes hold "editorial" meetings in the downstairs pub. "The fun of a pub is that you drop in on inspiration," he said in a 1988 interview. "It doesn't have to be planned."

352 If you frequent a drinking establishment that is dominated by a pool table, has a formica-top bar, or has a number in the name (such as "100 Club"), your drinking hole is not among the favourite drinking spots, according to the Bar Tourists of America. The group of 300 active members — men and women — conducts beer tasting forays across the United States in search of the perfect bar. It was formed in 1981 and they produce "official reports" on what to look for in a bar. They suggest that bars with men's names (Ben's, Al's) are good bets,as are places with "Haus" in the name. Bars with "Il," "El," "Le," or "La" are no good, they say, and bars with "Ye Olde" are hard to predict.

353 Robert M., of Toronto, was thirsty so he bought a case of beer. According to a report in the "crime news" of one of the city's newspapers, when he headed home through a laneway two men grabbed the beer and made their escape. Mr. M. went back to the beer store and bought another case.

As he stepped into the same laneway, the same two men grabbed the case of beer. "Not you again," he said. "Yes, and thanks," replied the two as they ran off once again. Mr. M. went home beerless. By that time the beer store had closed.

354 Working for a beer company has its advantages. The fringe benefits are great. At least that's what a man told his friends in Kitchener, Ontario, as he handed over case after case of beer—288 pints in all. The man said he had landed a job with Brewers Retail—Ontario's central beer distributing company—and that his friends could share in the benefits. None of his friends had qualms about accepting his largesse. Soon, however, the generous and very popular fellow was arrested for stealing a beer truck at a downtown intersection.

355 The Molson employee newsletter, *The Hopvine,* recounted this story: A Molson driver was on a long haul to Thunder Bay when he pulled his tractor-trailer onto the lot of a hotel in this northern Ontario city. During the night a thief broke into the trailer and stole 14 cases of beer. In his haste he neglectfully left his jacket in the trailer. Police were called and two police dogs were brought to the scene to sniff the jacket. Immediately, the dogs raced to the hotel and the burglar was caught standing at the bar drinking a Molson Export beer.

356 There are approximately 70,000 pubs in Britain and most are distinguished by a colourful, usually hand-painted sign out front designating the name, such as the Frog and the Nightgown, The Bird in Hand, or the Hansom Cab. Each pub's name is accompanied by an aptly drawn illustration.

One writer said Britain's inn signs are "a great open-air portrait gallery which covers the British Isles."

357 According to the *New York Times Magazine,* the father of microbrewing in the U.S. is Fritz Maytag, the creator of Anchor Steam Beer. He reopened the brewery of the old Steam Beer Brewing Company in San Francisco in 1965, initiating the small brewery revival. Writer Frank J. Prial said Maytag set the style for American microbreweries by turning out a variety of products and it is this diversity of style that is one of the reasons microbreweries and brewpubs have grown so popular.

358 In 14 years as a rough and tough hockey player with four National Hockey League teams, Dave "Tiger" Williams made mincemeat out of anybody foolish enough to tangle with him on the ice. The penalty-prone, hard-nosed tough guy also makes mincemeat in the kitchen, along with other types of food that contain beer in the recipes. Williams, who holds the all-time NHL penalty record with 3,873 minutes going into the 1987-88 season, is co-author of a book called *Done Like Dinner.* The book contains recipes for such tasty-sounding items as Eddie Shack's Beer-Baked Ham, Beer Fried Batter, Cheesy Beer Chowder, Cheddar Beer Spread and Spuds in Beer (that's potatoes, not the dog!).

359 Howard Collins of the Brewers Association of Canada said that 98% of the beer sold in Canada in 1987 was brewed in Canada. He added that beer is the country's most popular alcohol refreshment and it was consumed by 10 million Canadians that year.

360 The world's 2nd most popular beverage, next to tea, is beer, according to Bob Abel, author of *The Beer Book*. The globe-trotting journalist says he has travelled "a hard road, from non-discriminatory imbiber of beer to genteel quaffer to registered beerologist." He refers to pubs as "man's noblest institutions" while admitting that some are grubby while others are of considerable architectural interest. He maintains that a pub which offers flavourful beer and people to join in good talk, can be places to warm the heart and where cliches can come true. According to Abel, there's no better place than a pub to admire "the romance of beer in perhaps its fullest flowing." One of his favourite pubs is the Sun Inn on Lamb's Conduit Street, in London.

361 Advertisers in Buffalo, N.Y., reached out to captive male audiences by grabbing their attention in men's washrooms. In 1986, posters were displayed in the johns of 180 eateries and drinking spots throughout city. The campaign was called Tavern Talk and the messages were changed monthly. Sometimes jokes would appear on the posters. Bathroom humour, no doubt!

362 Frank Ansell worked in a beer store in Windsor, Ontario, in the 1920's, before the stores had refrigeration. In a 1987 interview, the 88-year-old former beer store manager recalled one memorable day in 1932: "The American Legion was meeting in Detroit and since the U.S. was dry at that time, the Legionnaires came across the border in search of beer. They arrived in boats, cars, and some brought carts and wagons with them. At our regular closing time (7 p.m.) there was still a line-up outside the beer store a quarter-mile long. We closed at 9:30 that night and sold $12,000 worth of beer in the last seven hours. That's when beer was $3.25 a case! One

Legionnaire was so happy, he gave me four medals that were pinned to his uniform."

363 Another "pioneer" of the Ontario brewing industry is Ena Johnson who remembers unloading beer trucks when she worked in a beer store on Toronto's Danforth Avenue in 1927. In a 1987 interview with *Kegs & Cases* magazine, Ena said she worked as a cashier in the store for 15 years but there were times when the store staff was away for lunch and she'd help unload the beer if a delivery truck arrived. She recalled the days when heavy canvas drapes were used to hide the store's beer stock to prevent the brewers from "jockeying for position." Those were also the days when many beer store windows were painted black to prevent people, especially youngsters, from peering in and becoming corrupted.

364 A curious belief of 12th century England credited beer with a greater durability than water when used for building purposes. The mortar used to hold the bricks together was often mixed with beer, especially when the work had to stand up to special strain, such as in a church steeple.

365 George Washington, the first president of the United States, enjoyed beer so much he had his own recipe. It appears on page six of the notebook he left when he was a Virginia Colonel in 1757. Here it is — and in his own words — straight from his notebook: "To make Small Beer — Take a large sifter full of Bran Hops to your taste — Boil these three hours, then strain out 30 gallons into a cooler. Put in 3 gallons molasses while the beer is scalding hot or rather draw the molasses into the cooler and strain the beer on it while boiling hot. Let these stand till it is little more than blood warm then put in a quart of yeast. If the weather is very cold cover it over with a blanket and let it work in the cooler 24 hours, then put it into a cask. Leave the bung open until it is almost done working — Bottle it that day-week it was brewed."

-END-

ABOUT THE AUTHOR

Dennis McCloskey has worked as a full-time writer and magazine editor since graduating in 1971 from Toronto's Ryerson Polytechnical Institute, where he earned a Journalism Degree.

Photo By Hal Sippel

A freelance editor of Brewers Retail's internal and external corporate magazines, his human interest articles have appeared in more than 25 newspapers and consumer and trade magazines, covering a variety of topics from skiing in northern British Columbia to a profile on the New York publisher of MAD magazine to the humour of politicians.

He is the author of two Young Adult fiction novels and co-inventor of the board game, Songsations.

Dennis lives in Richmond Hill, Ontario, with his wife, Kris, a Family Studies consultant with a Toronto school board.